Within Us

Within Us
© 2025 David Michael Kuhn
DavidKuhn.net

ISBN: 979-8-9902409-0-2

Published by Love Vibration Publications
First Edition, 2025

If you would like to teach directly from Within Us, we welcome
it! Please reference the book and author when quoting any
material. Thank you kindly.

Acknowledgements

A heartfelt thank you to Cat Hunter Shank, editor of Within Us. Your thoughtful care and insight have helped shape these words into something that flows with clarity and purpose. I am deeply grateful for your presence in this journey.

A special acknowledgement to Naomi Mulla. Your soulful presence shone brightly at a very pivotal time. I hold deep appreciation for the ways you've supported this process.

The herbal insights in this book are intended for educational and personal exploration. Plants have been recognized as our allies for millennia and yet each person's journey with them is unique. Please consult a trusted healthcare practitioner before working with these herbs, especially if you are pregnant, nursing, taking medications, or managing a health condition. Remember, we are always able to connect with the spirit of plants and receive their wisdom and medicine without physical ingestion. Listen to your body, move with intention, and trust your own experience.

Preface

Within Us serves as a companion guide to be revisited as a resource overtime. Written from the neutrality of Love, my intention is for readers to connect with the content from a place of neutrality. I chose to not include my personal stories of awakening for this reason; for the focus centers around your unique journey, not on mine.

This book is not meant to be intellectualized. Rather, the content is intended to be felt and embodied. It is not designed to be read in a conventional way—cover to cover, then set aside to collect dust. Instead, it is intended to be experienced as part of your personal awakening and support your process. The material offers a blueprint that resonates in neutrality—allowing you to internalize the material, as if the content emerged from you yourself. It can be easy to approach a book with the mindset of analyzing and remembering the content; however, the aim here is to move beyond that approach and allow the material to speak directly to your inner knowing. From this internalized and embodied state, you are invited to initiate the necessary changes and enter the—at times uncomfortable—state of growth and evolution.

Within Us carries a unique vibrational frequency. The book is designed to bring forth vibrational upgrades within the reader by simply being exposed to the words. You are encouraged to explore the material both individually and in community by talking about the subjects in a curious and expansive manner. It is not meant to serve as a rigid gospel or doctrine. Instead, it aims to spark inspiration and gently challenge beliefs rooted in separation. For this reason, it may not always align with your current belief system and thus feel foreign and even "edgy." This is an intentional component of the book to begin dismantling the old paradigm that lives on within us through our beliefs.

In speaking to people about the book throughout the writing process, I noticed something interesting... People often responded by referencing other writers' work instead of engaging directly with what I was saying—dismissal through comparison. It felt as though they were ending the conversation before it even began. I found this response to reflect the ego's tendency to convey that "I already know this material so I don't care nor need to consider this information." If you find yourself feeling uncomfortable or even thinking "I already know all of this stuff" as you read this book, it might be illuminating the very opposite—a sign to stay curious and carry on! It is important to recognize this for it can be an enlightenment trap—holding your ability to grow hostage by the ego.

I invite readers to not reject the information you have absorbed from books you have read or other sources you encountered. Instead, simply allow them to take a back seat so you are open to receive the new—maybe even foreign—concepts shared in this book. See how it feels for your inner knowing to guide you through the book versus the mind, see what may arise from within. Can you take my written words as mere inspiration for you to make *Within Us* your own—allow it to take root within you! Read it however feels right to you, maybe skip from chapter to chapter instead of reading it linearly from cover to cover. It can be a great exercise of listening to our inner knowing—our guidance system beyond the rational mind—to flip through a book, stop when you feel called, and then go to the beginning of the chapter you opened and read from there. I often find the content to be strikingly accurate and resonant with whatever is moving through my life at that time—a type of oracle.

Likewise, return to the book as needed and notice how the meanings and explanations may evolve alongside you. Practice the suggestions and meditations, but remember, this book is merely a guidepost for your own awakening. This book encourages the reader to release what they have learned under the separation paradigm and how our current society has indoctrinated us with certain narratives and beliefs that further the illusion of separation. Simultaneously, the book invites you to cultivate and strengthen your inner knowing and form new beliefs that support an expansive, creative, and abundant life far beyond the limitations of our current reality. How this material is integrated or inspires your journey is entirely unique to you—allow the content to work for you, make it your own!

As you read, pay attention to what does not resonate. If you feel stuck or have a strong resistance to something, take a look at why you feel stuck and why it does not resonate... there may be a key hiding in it. Nothing in this book seeks or intends to cause harm. May you feel safe and held by the nourishment of Love as you traverse the varied landscape of this book.

I recommend skipping the "sticky" parts and returning to them later, rather than pausing on the book entirely. While *Within Us* is not a conventional story, the "plot" is structured to build upon itself—paralleling the evolutionary journey.

After rereading and rewriting this book many times over the last three years" I still find it inspiring and revealing to revisit chapters. Each time I do, something new awakens within me—and I wrote the book! This is because we are constantly evolving and therefore revisit the information from a new vantage point.

Within Us came to be through Divine inspiration. At times it was easeful and in flow to align with and follow these guidelines, often it was challenging to live it and write it. During the COVID-19 pandemic in 2020, I felt pulled to Taos, New Mexico, a place I had briefly visited before. Following this intuition, I left Vermont after publishing my first book that detailed my personal journey navigating the early stages of awakening. After moving to Taos I experienced the Divinely guided chaotic nodes of awakening—the potent cycles of collapse and rebuilding on faith. I was not intending to co-create another book, but was given clear guidance that another book was to be born detailing the impersonal, collective process of awakening. The communication to write *Within Us* offered clear directives to make it accessible to a wide audience by not including personal stories or mention of specific governments or religions. While I briefly touch on these topics for context, the essence of the book remains neutral for readers to experience and embody the material in their own way.

When I began writing, I did not have a clear sense of how the book would start or end or even the arch of the content. I intentionally avoided outside influences, steering clear of YouTube videos or other materials related to the topics I was exploring. Writing this book often felt like a leap of faith into the unknown, which interestingly is a central component of the evolutionary journey we are all on or embarking on. Much of the writing process felt like a transmission, a download of information. Material often came to me in dreams, rarely through the logical planning mind. There were times I doubted myself, feeling like a fraud as the words seemed to surpass my own level of understanding and embodiment. For instance, I have not studied quantum physics and yet these concepts—these truths—came through me to be woven into the book. Nevertheless, as I wrote each chapter it would begin to manifest—to come alive—in my life, offering me direct lessons through tangible experiences.

There were numerous challenging and unforeseen side effects throughout the creation process. For example, I was interestingly immersed in darker environments to serve others working with the unhoused population and those struggling with addiction. Paradoxically, it often felt as though I was attracting lower vibrational energies while writing content that resonates at a much higher frequency. I also gained weight during the process and see it as a result of my body not yet being ready to embody aspects of the material and therefore physically insulating and protecting the system. While challenging at times, these experiences served to counterbalance and illuminate the profound energies that were flowing through me.

Ironically, the very notion that I was channeling something beyond myself to write this book is rooted in a separation-based belief system and thus is not entirely accurate. To balance this, it felt imperative to remember that the information moving through me was not exclusive—it is accessible to anyone who is open to receive. This is not a matter of being more "awake" or "chosen." Rather, it is simply part of my soul's destined purpose to bring forth this work so others may also access and embody this Unity knowledge in their own, Divine way. Understanding that I am no different than any other human being and that all hierarchy is a construct is key and a foundational Unity belief. That said, of course I am "special" and so is each of us, each life form, each element of creation!

Writing this book was the ultimate practice of trust. Each time I revisited the material, I realized the material was in fact authentic regardless of my doubting mind. I often asked, "Why me? Why would someone as flawed as I am be writing something so Divine?" In time the answer came, "You are Divine. You are worthy." My lack of formal education, reputation, and complex authenticity made me the perfect vessel for this manuscript. I had nothing to lose; my life had already fallen apart. I had only an old truck and my son, who lived with me part-time. Although I had studied in depth the science of vibration, shamanism, psychosynthesis and herbalism and been offering regular sound healing ceremonies and working with clients 1:1, I had stopped all of this. I felt lost and unsure of where or how to begin again.

The process of creating *Within Us* with Divine inspiration gave my life meaning every day, uplifting me from the darkest moments over the last few years. Even when I didn't fully believe what I was writing, it felt unwaveringly safe and real. I found myself rewriting the book numerous times—allowing it to grow as I grew. I dove into the book until my resources ran out, took jobs here and there to support myself during the depths of my creative hibernation.

Remarkably—Divinely—each time finances ran dry I was given an unexpected opportunity, witnessing and experiencing the truth that we are always protected and provided for when living in trust. Relationships fell away, leaving me alone for much of the writing process. Over time, I realized this book was my purpose, which in turn served as the catalyst for my own shift into Unity.

The final rewrites wove everything together in perfect Unity. I learned how to express and verbalize the concepts as well as integrate the lived experiences that made these vibrational upgrades so impactful. True change does not come from regurgitating external concepts, but from embodying what resonates deeply within us. Most books carry the codes to a collective upgrade and can shift various perspectives of the reader. *Within Us* is no different and might even go deeper with the direct invitations to consciously release and adopt a new paradigm—letting old worn out beliefs blow away and allow new seeds of Unity to take root in the soil of your body, embracing the wisdom and guidance of your inner knowing.

In this process, like anything in life, we must begin exactly where we are. You are Divine and worthy of awakening, no matter what you've done or who you believe an enlightened being "should" be. You can embrace your authentically perfect imperfections, while also holding a higher vibration. In fact, the act of acknowledging and embracing carries a much higher frequency than that of denying and repressing. No need to let your inner critic convince you that you're not good enough, this is far from the truth and merely a manifestation of separation beliefs. It is time to honor and embody the Divine, eternal light of your soul.

Enjoy and explore the pages of *Within Us* at your own pace—page by page, returning to various sections or practices as needed. It is my wish that this book will hold and support you, as it has lovingly done for me. Allow the strong vibration to stoke your inner light and guide you forward. If you feel stuck, don't give up—keep reading, keep growing. It may sound cliché... but trust the process. The path of awakening, like all of nature, does not function as a straight line. And yet the meandering and bumpy path has a long, clear trajectory of wakefulness. May you find refuge and hope as the content lifts the veil of illusion and welcomes you into the Divine portal of the unknown. Standing on the threshold of a new paradigm, we will aid the collective awakening of humanity—together, in Unity.

With Love,
David

Within Us

Table of Contents

Chapter One- Within Us 1

Chapter Two- The Spark 15

Chapter Three- Neutrality 29

Chapter Four- Elemental Patterns 39

Chapter Five- Beliefs 55

Chapter Six- Abundance 73

Chapter Seven- The Living Earth 87

Chapter Eight- Unity Language 101

Chapter Nine- Ancestral Lineage 119

Chapter Ten- We Are Not Alone 131

Chapter Eleven- Shadow 147

Chapter Twelve- Embodiment 169

Chapter Thirteen- Joy 189

Chapter Fourteen- Sexuality 193

Chapter Fifteen- Love Vibration 207

Chapter Sixteen- Natural Algorithms 217

Chapter Seventeen- Gateways 233

Chapter Eighteen- The One Timeline 243

Chapter Nineteen- The Quantum Human 257

Chapter Twenty- The Golden Timeline 267

Key Terms & Concepts 283
Reading List 289

CHAPTER ONE

WITHIN US

WE HOLD THE ORIGIN SEED TO UNITY WITHIN US

We are in the midst of an unprecedented evolutionary leap. We are not broken—we are rising. We are not insane—we are waking up. This pervasive shift has been prophesied. We are becoming the masters we have been waiting for. At our core lies a strength, a force beyond all external influence.

How is this possible?

Within each of us lies the origin seed of Unity. This seed carries the genetic blueprint for the unfolding of our true nature. Imprinted within us is a vibrational signature that is unique to our individual and collective purpose. This blueprint contains evolutionary codes embedded within us. These genetic codes are now being activated.

Learning to trust in the process of awakening
is the same as learning to trust ourselves.

This miraculous metamorphosis is already underway. It is not tied to a specific religious dogma, race, socioeconomic structure, or government system. The intrinsic beauty of this awakening cannot be stopped, for it arises from within us. While we each experience
unique journeys, we are all moving toward a paradigm shift of epic proportion. We currently live within and participate in an upside-down reality where the biological operating systems that we rely on were built upon the illusion of separation.

What we are experiencing—both individually and collectively—can be compared to the metamorphosis of a butterfly. On the other side of this vibrational shift, we will not be the same. Our perceptions and beliefs will transform, and the ways we interact, work, and play will change as well. Everything—from our internal thoughts to our sense of purpose—will undergo a profound transfiguration. This personal transformation will ripple outward, becoming a collective metamorphosis for us all.

Like the caterpillar, we are being called to surrender to a process of transformation—a personal and collective cocooning, so to speak. This process is unstoppable. The information we need to navigate this shift already exists within us and as we step into this state of remembering, we learn to trust our awakened inner knowing. Likewise, the caterpillar embarks on an incredible journey, trusting the process as they transform from a caterpillar into a cocoon and then into a butterfly. This transformation is not simply about change—it is about fully releasing the former self. After evolving, the butterfly's reality is entirely different—a complete metamorphosis has occurred, unleashing ultimate freedom. The caterpillar likely does not understand what is happening while the transformation is underway, nor are they

directing the process. Rather, by implicitly trusting their Divine inner knowing, the evolution happens to them—within them.Protected by the genetic remembering from those who have gone before, the caterpillar surrenders and is given wings.We too carry a genetic memory embedded in our inner knowing. These instilled genetic markers are currently being vibrationally activated. The enlightened ascended masters who were the first to experience Unity, gifted us the Origin seed of Unity—sowing the path to Unity within us.

Just as the caterpillar instinctively knows to build a cocoon and undergo metamorphosis, we too may sense that something within us is changing. While we are not building a literal cocoon, we are entering a mirrored process—creating a safe space where we can transmute our belief systems and shift our reality from the illusion of separation into Unity.

Just as the caterpillar surrenders to the mystery within their cocoon, we are being called to confront the systemic fear that lives within us and release outdated beliefs and identities. This process—the death of what we once knew—demands the courageous act of stepping into the unknown. The caterpillar's disintegration into a seemingly lifeless state is a powerful reminder that facing the deeply seeded fear of transformation is an essential part of growth. It is only through this symbolic death that true emergence is possible.

This book explores ways to support the journey through the awakening process by fostering awareness, acceptance, and a willingness to navigate these changing waters—leaping into the unknown. Like the butterfly who emerges renewed and whole, we are rediscovering our true nature, learning to trust in our inner knowing and embrace the unfolding of a new paradigm.

Before we traverse any further:
What is a paradigm?
What is the illusion of separation?
What is a Unity paradigm?

A paradigm is a framework or model that shapes how we perceive, understand, and interpret the world around us. It includes the beliefs, assumptions, values, and practices that guide the way individuals, groups, or societies think and act.

In philosophy, a paradigm represents an overarching worldview or perspective that informs how we make sense of reality. For example, shifting from seeing the Earth as flat to understanding it as a sphere was a major change in human thought. In science, a paradigm is an accepted body of theories and practices within a field. When new discoveries fundamentally challenge existing theories, they can lead to a "paradigm shift," such as the transition from Newtonian physics to Einstein's theory of relativity.

Socially and culturally, paradigms represent the dominant ways of thinking or living during a particular time period, such as the transition from an industrial society to a digital one. On a personal level, paradigm shifts involve vibrational changes that dissolve limiting beliefs, reshaping the mental frameworks through which we see ourselves and our lives. Shifting a personal paradigm might mean moving from a mindset of scarcity to one of abundance, opening the door to new possibilities and ways of being.

A paradigm shift happens when fundamental assumptions or beliefs are overturned, revealing new ways of thinking and operating. These shifts are evolutionary and foster growth, innovation, and transformation, creating new possibilities for perception and experience. We are currently experiencing a frozen paradigm where the evolutionary process has stagnated, thereby increasing entropy. Greater entropy both increases heat and slows the evolutionary process. This is the grave byproduct of the veil of illusion.

The illusion of separation is an energetic field that has woven itself into our belief systems, creating a fear-based veil that disconnects us from one another, from nature, and from our Divine self. This perception is systemic in the body and can foster a sense of isolation and disempowerment, which then fuels oppression, unhealthy competition, division, and fear. It serves as the foundation for many societal paradigms that prioritize individuality at the cost of unhealthy separation or in some cultures, oppressive fascism. The foundational underlying belief in scarcity—not connection and abundance—perpetuates disconnection and limits our potential for Unity and harmony.

The paradigm shift we all are currently experiencing is dismantling the illusion of separation and revealing the truth of our interconnectedness. As we move from a paradigm of separation to one of Unity, we begin to see how we are creating our own reality. We begin to experience an increased flow in energy and abundance. The unraveling of the separation paradigm is happening within us and is exponential. The difference now, compared to previous paradigm shifts, is that rather than emerging externally it is blooming from within us. For this reason, it cannot be stopped.

Creating harmony during this collective shift is ultimately a matter of choice. As we awaken to the changes unfolding within us, we gain greater access to tools and practices that can ease the transition. The simple act of recognizing that we are all venturing into the unknown marks a significant part of the journey.

For inspiration, we can look to those who have already transitioned into the one-timeline—individuals whose paths remind us that stepping into the unknown brings about a profound transformation. Like a butterfly emerging from their cocoon, we undergo a metamorphosis that leads to newfound freedom, lightness, and alignment with our true nature.

This book serves as a detailed blueprint,
offering tools and insights to guide and ease the transition
into the unknown—into the Unity paradigm.

Learning to take courageous leaps into the unknown—toward Unity—despite the unease it may bring, is one of the most transformative skills we can develop. By stepping from passivity into active participation, we align ourselves with the ascension process. Every intentional choice to ride the vibrational waves of the unknown lifts us into new frequencies and opens the door to greater purpose, abundance, and fulfillment. On this journey, we discover a liberating freedom anchored in trust. As our inner vibration rises higher and higher, we begin to recognize that external validation loses its weight and is replaced by a quiet, steady sense of wholeness that arises from within.

The journey to Unity is a series of frequency shifts that arise from the planet, the sun, and from within us. In between these frequency shifts, we encounter what is known as a chaotic node—a period of turbulence as our entire system integrates the changes. This chaotic node is the experience of the unknown. It is the space where we feel disoriented, uncomfortable, and unsure of what lies ahead.

These chaotic nodes are necessary for reconfiguring our belief structures, all the way down to the cellular level. Each time we move through one of these nodes, we reach the other side with a deeper understanding and learn that there was never anything to fear. This process creates recognizable patterns in our awakening, revealing that what once felt overwhelming is actually an invitation to evolve.

From this place of self-awareness, we begin to move through chaotic nodes with greater ease, trusting the process rather than resisting it. We can also observe this phenomenon on a collective level as humanity undergoes its own shared vibrational shifts. The turbulence we experience as a whole reflects the same reconfiguration process we experience as individuals, reminding us that the path to Unity is one of transformation—an unfolding where the unknown becomes a gateway rather than a barrier.

Unity does not mean the absence of duality; rather, it represents the emergence of balanced polarity within us. In many ways, Unity is a return to the harmonious integration of feminine and masculine energies. From this equilibrium, a new, abundant reality begins to take shape. The spark of Unity ignites a shift within each of us, laying the foundation for a transformative new paradigm.

The illusion of separation has long distorted the natural flow of equality—the balanced and clear reflection of our true nature. From this imbalanced place, inequality has run rampant on Earth. When we begin to experience an inner equanimity, we will recognize the roots of the Unity paradigm are taking hold. This is the paradigm shift!

Many of us find comfort in the familiar, clinging to what we know as a way to create a sense of safety in a world that often feels uncertain. These roles, habits, and places that we have long inhabited can act as anchors and give us the illusion of stability. The familiar soothes us, offering predictable routines in a landscape that appears unpredictable or unsafe. While this may feel comforting, it can also serve as a barrier to growth and transformation.

The very routines that feel safe may, in reality, be keeping us tethered to the illusion of separation. By staying within the confines of these patterns, we reinforce a paradigm that resists change and limits our ability to embrace new possibilities. This resistance can make the transition to Unity—a state of interconnectedness and balance—much more challenging. The more we hold on, the harder it becomes to let go of the old frameworks that no longer serve us.

Unity requires stepping into a new way of being—a space where familiar structures dissolve and new beliefs systems take hold to guide us. Imagine a reality where we feel abundant and safe and can embody our true nature—a healthy, creative state of equanimity. From this vibration, the external reality begins to shift. When the individuals leading government, educational, and healthcare systems experience this shift, we will see these structures rapidly change from within—mirroring the evolution occurring within each of us.

It can be challenging to see beyond what we are experiencing in the here and now. It may be difficult to imagine healing the core wounds of our culture, let alone restoring health to our planet. The only way we will be able to envision such a paradigm shift is if it first happens within us. When we start experiencing this shift ourselves, it all begins to make a bit more sense. Letting go of the familiar does not mean abandoning safety; rather, it invites us to find a deeper sense of safety within ourselves—one rooted in trust and alignment with the greater whole. It is in this surrender that we begin to experience the freedom and expansiveness of Unity and discover the profound connection that has been waiting for us beyond the confines and comfort of the "known." The structures—both internal and external—that we are accustomed to manifesting from and living within can be likened to a birdcage. A bird, having never known any other way of life, accepts their existence within the cage and finds contentment in the familiarity. One day, however, the cage is moved to a meadow and left there with the door propped open. For the first time, the bird is faced with the possibility of stepping into an utterly new world. Accustomed to the perceived safety of their cage, the bird watches the wonders of nature from the "safe" space. However, as the food supply within the cage dwindles, the bird is compelled to venture beyond the familiar enclosure in search of nourishment. This brave step into the unknown leads to an extraordinary discovery—a newfound freedom and a life the bird had never even imagined. At first, the bird may return to the cage, drawn back by familiar comfort. Yet, over time, the notion of the cage being "safe" starts to fade as the bird realizes that the cage in fact is a limitation to their existence. In time, the bird fully embraces this new life, leaving the cage behind—soar through the open sky, returning to the boundless beauty and freedom of nature. This story serves as a simple metaphor for our current choice.

The door to Unity stands open before us...

Do we choose to embrace our true nature? Or, do we wait until circumstances force our hand?

When do we step through the door to embrace our best life? Is it possible to leave and return? Or, must we simply take flight and trust the purposeful wind to guide us?

It is our fear and the accompanying resistance that pose the greatest challenges in our birthing process. Learning to make clear, intentional choices that align with our inner knowing requires us to trust what we do not yet know—a process that can take time. Beyond the illusion of separation there is clear, authentic messaging. We are accustomed to receiving information that has been filtered through the lackluster lens of illusion. Lifetimes of programming have distorted our Divinity and inner knowing, feeding us skewed information tainted by scarcity. This is why it can be challenging to hear and trust our inner knowing. As a result, we tend to rely on external sources to make decisions, causing our inner knowing to atrophy, leaving us drained and disempowered.

What is one thing we can do today that feels uncomfortable? Facing our fears can start with small actions that push us beyond our comfort zones. For instance, sitting in silence for a few minutes every hour; engaging in a friendly conversation with a stranger; listening to a new genre of music without immediate judgement. While these may seem overly simple, they can pave the path for sustainable growth. We are all different and therefore have unique fears to explore. Leap in!

The profound shift to choose
Love over fear is accessible to everyone.
In orienting to Love—to acceptance—in all moments,
we begin to sense the frequency of Unity that gently lifts the
veil of illusion & dissolves separation.

As we look around at the world we live in, it is easy to believe there is no way we all will wake up. It can be tempting to think it's too late for us... too late to shift into Unity... too late to save the ecosystem. The dominant narrative we encounter tends to be one of negative resignation. In turn, it can be challenging to remember—let alone wholeheartedly believe—that we possess the power to alter and initiate both individual and collective change within us!

While there is certainly a case to be made that we are doomed—that the ecosystem will not regenerate as long as humans remain on Earth or that humanity's true nature is rooted in greed and violence. It is easy to look at history and fall into despair, overwhelmed by "whataboutisms" and defeatism. However, these notions only inhibit change. It is the narrative of a dying paradigm and ultimately an illusion.

Imagine a meadow of wildflowers swaying in a gentle breeze. From a distance, the field appears to be a single, unified color. However, in drawing nearer, the intricate complexity of the field is revealed. Each flower uniquely expresses themselves in

Divine timing—some have bloomed, while others wait for the perfect moment to unfurl. What causes certain flowers to bloom first? Why do others wait until the last moment to reveal their beauty?

The answer is simple. They bloom when they are ready!

Each flower has a purpose that is just as important as the next and buds are just as worthy as flowers in full bloom.

Those who bloom first simply serve as catalysts, inspiring those nearby to open their petals to the sun. Like the flowers, we are each perfectly Divine right where we are, just as we are, and are all destined to bloom—to awaken—in due timing. Just as we cannot force a flower to open before the destined time, we cannot alter the timeline of our evolution. No matter where we are in the blooming process, our light shines brightly. We are beautiful and complete in every moment, no matter the conditions!

Once we taste the nectar of Unity,
like the hummingbird, we return joyfully for more.

Herbal Insights: Blue Lotus *(Nymphaea caerulea)*

Blue Lotus has been used historically for its mild psychoactive effects and was considered sacred in Ancient Egypt. It contains apomorphine and nuciferine, which can promote relaxation and dream-like states. Blue Lotus is often associated with moments of awakening and brings ease during times of transformation.

Enjoy in tea, tincture, or can be smoked.

CHAPTER TWO

THE SPARK

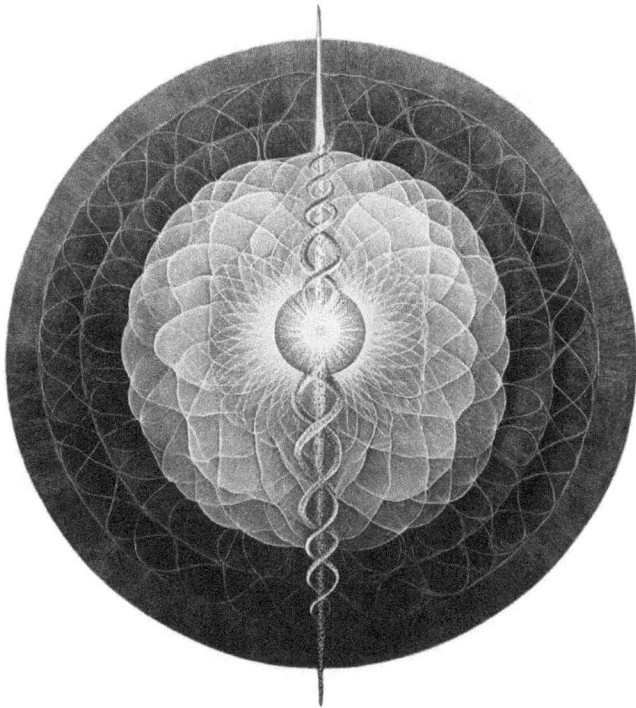

*ALL CREATION IS BORN FROM THE SPARK
OF POLARITY, IN DIVINE UNION*

To provide a fundamental baseline of understanding of how we are interconnected and to ground us in the pragmatic, let's explore the Unified field of potentiality.

Humans Embody the most advanced operating system, far surpassing any digital technology we have created to date. At the center of all life lies an electromagnetic structure known as a toroidal field. This torus, a donut-like shape, represents the fundamental energetic architecture from which all life emerges.

This energetic structure allows for a continuous flow of energy, simultaneously receiving and transmitting information. This interaction creates a unified field of interconnected energy. The field has been described in many ways—toroidal field, morphogenetic field, biofield, and energy body. Regardless of the given name, the phenomena illuminates in the interwoven tapestry and constant communication between all life forms.

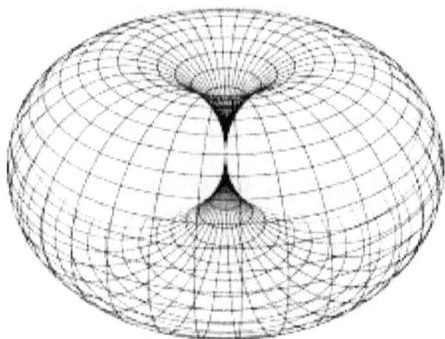

The toroidal field is more than a simple electromagnetic field. While the movement of ions and electrical charges forms a basis, the torus is a self-organizing and dynamic system, where energy spirals from the core and returns, thus creating a constant balance. This continuous flow of energy aligns with concepts in quantum physics, namely quantum entanglement and non-locality, where particles remain connected across space and time. The energy within the torus also correlates with the idea of zero-point energy—the quantum vacuum state from which all energy flows.

This zero-point energy is the neutrality of love, where pure love resides—ecstatic, expansive, nourishing, and all-knowing. Often named God, Creator, Spirit, Source energy. This energy is not separate from us; rather, it is the origin from which we emerge. The neutrality of love is where all information converges; it is the nucleus of creation. This energy creates and sustains life from a place of love that is all knowing. and is constantly moving with intention in the ebb and flow of receiving and giving.

The neutrality of love resides in every life form, thus serving to intimately connect all life. If a single place existed where we could point and say God lives here, this would be the place. But the reality is this source of energy is in and creates everything, We are not in separation from it. God is not some external force that resides in heaven, it is not a he or a she. We are created to co-create in God's likeness. When we pray the thoughts and words are heard in the neutrality of love. Our prayers are answered in the most unexplainable ways through the web of life's interconnectedness.

Love's sole desire is for every facet of creation—of life—to grow and evolve in harmony.

Research in bioelectromagnetism has demonstrated that the cells within our bodies produce their own electromagnetic fields. These fields influence processes such as cell division, healing, and inter-cell communication. Epigenetic studies have shown that environmental factors, including electromagnetic fields, can alter gene expression. From this we can conclude that strong vibrational ascension waves hitting our bodies can alter DNA and genetic coding that lead to evolutionary timeline jumping,

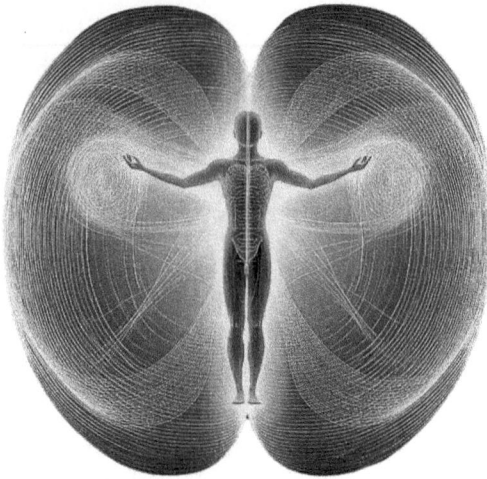

The toroidal field in humans mirrors the Earth's geomagnetic field and the heart's electromagnetic field, thus suggesting that all living systems are part of one energetic ecosystem where constant communication and information transfers within everything all the time.

For example: A salamander has the same toroidal field as everything else and whatever information it receives with its senses is recorded into the unified field and is then accessible to all life. All information from all life forms is processed the same way. The toroidal field occurs on all scales—micro to macro—from the electromagnetic field surrounding each human cell; to the electromagnetic field radiating from the heart; to the Earth's geomagnetic field. Recent research in bioelectromagnetism reifies that all life is part of and co-creates an energetic ecosystem.

With this understanding we are able to acknowledge our innate connection with all life—on and beyond Earth. We are related to all life forms in all dimensions of the universe through the toroidal field surrounding each of us. Since all life forms create this flow of energy, we are capable of communicating with any and all life forms!

18

The quantum field encompasses a symphony of subtle energies, vibrational frequencies, and consciousness fields. Every living being contributes to this intricate energetic tapestry, forming a collective field of consciousness that both informs our individual and collective experiences. While modern science is shedding light on certain phenomena and increasing our awareness of the unseen energetic realms, the beauty and complexity of life's interconnectedness reaches far beyond what science can explain.

To fully honor the magnitude and mystery of the operating system within us, we must first acknowledge we have been living in a paradigm that promotes the illusion of separation. The lens of separation limits our perception to a narrow portion of reality, thus diminishing the potential power within us. As we begin to embody the essence of Unity, we gradually shed the programming that has led us into the illusion of separation. By grounding into the taproot of the Unity paradigm rising we may begin to experience how the toroidal field system in our body is capable of quantum computation and how this capacity is further enhanced by our conscious participation. In returning to Unity, we return to the infinite pool of potential and information that exists within us.

The Spark of polarity—of feminine & masculine energy— coupled with the Unity of Divine Love, creates the Origin seeds for all life.

In the center of the toroidal field feminine and masculine energies merge. Nourished by the neutrality of love, their union sparks the creation of life. This spark is the birthplace of all existence. Within this spark, Unity emerges and the cyclical rhythm of love flows freely, thus feeding the torus.

The creative force sparked by the union of feminine and masculine energies isn't only about the physical connection between a man and a woman. Instead, it's about seeing these energies as deeply inherent and more essential than outward forms. While this union is one way the spark of creation—of Unity—appears, these opposite energies constantly combine in countless ways, creating everything from ideas to animals to plants to the solar system in which we live

Due to the expansive nature of Unity, at the very moment of the spark—of Union—the toroidal field undergoes a significant expansion. This field, which surrounds and connects all forms of life, rapidly swells outward, symbolizing the boundless nature of creation. Yet, just as swiftly as it expands, a powerful contraction follows, drawing the energy field back into its core. It is through this cyclical rhythm—of expansion and contraction—that energy is both sustained and created. This continuous pulsation forms the heartbeat of existence, a dynamic flow that generates life and maintains its vibrancy across all layers of reality.

As the Unity paradigm continues to take root, we will be able to harness the power of the toroidal field system—accessing the neutrality of love—accessing free and abundant energy to power everything with neither wires nor waste.

Those who are able to see the unified field describe it as a geometric grid, compared to a honeycomb design. This pattern permeates all boundaries and is present in all life, from seemingly inanimate matter to sentient beings to the foundational elements. This luminous pulsating grid is alive—full of and created by energy. As a living, breathing, fractalized matrix, the grid is ever evolving creating Origin seeds that will birth more toroidal fields.

The inception of the universe, often referred to as the Big Bang, mirrors all other sparks of creation and simply occurred at the macro level.

When a plant seed forms, it signifies the spark of creation. The Origin seeds carry all genetic information and the energetic blueprint for the crystalline structure that will take form during germination. This crystalline structure is established well before the physical plant starts to sprout, it is the cosmic blueprint for creation.

All seeds—whether they belong to plants, animals, the universe, or even the seed of an idea or a Unity paradigm—are born through the same fundamental process. Before a seed grows into an expanded physical form, a crystalline structure emerges, born amid the neutrality of love from the spark of Unity. This crystalline structure serves as a guide for growth while simultaneously reflecting the dimensional frequency that brought it into existence, reminding the emerging being of their Divine origin. Each frequency carries a distinct mathematical pattern and signature, forming a sacred geometry. The crystalline structures are inherently masculine, representing the stable framework from which feminine energy—the creative force—can breathe life into this seed of creation. The feminine requires a structure to manifest, while the masculine structure remains inert without the enlivening touch of the feminine.

This intricate dance of life, of creation, unfolds within us,
harmonized by the grace of pure, neutral love.

The Origin seed of Unity consciousness was co-created by two awakened humans sharing in a divine union. Over millennia, this seed has been nurtured, growing from its crystalline structure into a sprout that now lives within each of us. As the spark progresses, entering the Unity paradigm phase, we make strides from the conceptualization to the embodiment of Unity consciousness. Unity consciousness manifests as a unique energetic field, anchored in the Earth's heart, our hearts, and in the vast heart of the universe.

The unified field forms an immense toroidal structure interconnected with all other toroidal fields—there is no separation, only a unified collective. This is the Universal Mind, feminine in nature, flowing seamlessly through these fields. As it moves, it creates sparks of energy in dynamic interplay with the masculine energy. These sparks serve as the inception of all life, the very essence of creation itself.

There are eleven dimensions within this Unified field representing the quantum field of pure potential. Each dimension carries a unique frequency, forming a complex and intricate system. As we move toward the fifth dimension, a vibrational shift occurs. This shift initiates the individual state of Unity, which in turn supports the Unity Paradigm in being established for the collective.

This is why many humans have begun to notice the number 11:11, as it is a code for Unity. When we see it, it reminds us that Unity is within us and that we are on the path to embodying its vibration. 11:11 also symbolizes the eleven dimensions and the highest form of communication in our universe, which dwells in the eleventh dimension.

The illusion of separation arises from the belief that our reality is singular, as if we exist in a fixed, linear system like a digital computation. This view leads us to believe that our experiences are isolated, disconnected from the larger web of existence. Quantum entanglement research however fundamentally challenges this notion demonstrating that particles who were once connected remain linked across time and space, regardless of distance. While fundamental and even rudimentary, this finding is just the beginning of revealing deeper truths that many of humans and cultures have long sensed to be true—we are not separate beings, rather we are interconnected with all life and all realities, all at once.

For many individuals, this understanding may have always been present, though we struggled to find adequate language to describe it. The belief that everything is interconnected—that thoughts, actions, and events ripple across the universe and manifest our reality—has existed in ancient spiritual traditions for centuries. Modern science however, has been slow to embrace these concepts. Certain intuitive understandings about the nature of reality have been dismissed and labeled as pseudoscience. For instance, the reduction of synchronicities to being random coincidences.

Synchronicities—the meaningful connections and patterns that emerge in life—are far more than random. They serve as indicators of the underlying Unity between all things, a reflection of the quantum field that connects us all. As we deepen our understanding of quantum entanglement and consciousness, we begin to see that life is not a series of disconnected events, but a continuous exchange of energy, constantly evolving in harmony with the greater whole.

We are not consumers.
We are energy exchangers.
We are co-creators.

Unified Hearts Meditation

is a practice that explores the cultivation of love, compassion, and connection. This meditation offers an opportunity to unify the feminine and masculine energies that dwell in the heart and thus spark the co-creative essence of love.

First Heart – Inner Heart

Bring your awareness to the heartspace. Feel your breath fill this place, creating spaciousness and warmth. Notice if this fosters a pleasant sensation. If so, maybe wear a soft smile—feeling appreciation for this breath.

Another avenue to stoke the flame within the inner heart may be to recall a memory of a place, or connection—human or beyond—that is imbued with love and thus evokes the felt sense of love within you. Allow yourself to fully immerse in

this sensation, growing gratitude as we consciously recognize
how love feels in the body.

Second Heart – Earth Heart

Shift your attention to where your body touches the chair or
ground beneath you. Feel gravity pulling you to the heart of
the Earth. Maintaining this connection to the Earth's core,
bring awareness back to your own heart. Explore the
connection between the heart in your chest and the heart of
the Earth. Maybe your meditation remains in the somatic
realm as a felt sense. Or you may visualize a beam of light, or a
thread of energy, connecting the two hearts. As you inhale,
draw energy up from the Earth's core into your center, feeling
the innate connection. On the out breath, offer your love and
gratitude back to the Earth.

Third Heart – Cosmic Heart

Bring your awareness upward—above your head—and imagine
a third heart. This is the cosmic heart. Establish a connection
between your physical inner heart and the cosmic heart.
Again, you might sense this connection as a beam of light, a
flow of energy, or a felt sense. Breathe in, drawing the light
and wisdom of the cosmic heart into your own. As you exhale,
release your energy upward, sharing your unique light and
inner knowing with the cosmos. Remain in this exchange,
sensing your connection with all life.

Unifying the Three Hearts

Allow each breath to strengthen the connection between the
heart of the Earth, your inner heart, and the cosmic heart. Feel
the flow of love, light, and energy between the three hearts.

Take refuge and find rest in this integrated state of being, in Unity.

Closing the Meditation

Gradually bring your attention back to your physical heart. Allow your breath to return to its own rhythm. Feel the body breathe itself. Rest in the peace you have cultivated. When you feel complete, gently open your eyes, returning to your surroundings while maintaining the harmony of the three hearts within you.

Meditation is deeply personal. Please use this as inspiration, adjusting it to best support you. What matters most is the intention behind the practice—feeling connectivity and love and remembering we each carry the potential to cultivate these feeling states internally, regardless of our outer world.

Herbal Insights - Motherwort

Motherwort (*Leonurus cardiaca*) strengthens the physical heart while offering deep comfort during times of transition. Used for centuries in traditional medicine, this steadfast herb provides steady support as emotions rise and shift. With her gentle yet unwavering presence, she creates space to feel, process, and embrace the depth of our inner world.

Ways to Connect with Motherwort
  ☽ **Tea & Tincture** – The most common methods for internal use.
  ☽ **Energetic & Emotional Support** – Engaging with motherwort through **meditation**, ritual, or simply sitting with the plant can foster a deep sense of calm and resilience.

Cacao (*Theobroma cacao*) has long been used in sacred ceremony, known for its ability to open the heart and deepen connection. Whether shared in community or in quiet solitude, cacao invites warmth, clarity, and expansion.

Ways to Connect with Cacao
  ☽ **Ceremonial Preparation** – Brew organic ceremonial cacao with intention, creating space for reflection and heart-centered awareness.
  ☽ **Sacred Ritual** – Sit with cacao, breathing in its essence. Allow its energy to move through you, guiding you into deeper connection and openness. Then, gently take a sip.

The heart beyond the heart, the love beyond the love—suspended in the weightlessness of a wish for wholeness. Through the tangled mess of life, we come to see that the mess itself is the gift. Love, untamed and immeasurable, flows freely. And that is the gift of love, the gift of the heart.

CHAPTER THREE

NEUTRALITY

THE POINT OF SURRENDER AND WHERE MYSTICAL
DIVINITY BEGINS—THE PAUSE BETWEEN TWO ACTIONS.
FIND COMFORT & TAKE REFUGE HERE.

Everything is created in the neutrality of love. Thus it makes perfect sense that we are nourished by returning to this place. When we embrace neutrality, we experience moments of clarity that allow the divine to flow freely through us, opening the way for new perspectives to arise.

Embracing neutrality does not equate to doing nothing. Rather, the energy of neutrality embodies action: sharp clarity, heightened intuition, and potent synchronicities—all of which align the universe in our favor!

From early on, we are conditioned to perceive the world through narrow dichotomies: virtue and vice, angels and demons. This duality is reflected in our literature, films, and folklore where heroes combat villains. We come to believe that there is always an enemy that we must protect ourselves from.

The art of neutrality takes practice as it contradicts everything we have been taught. Neutrality paves the road home to our true nature, offering a sanctuary of serenity and simplicity. It is a state of equanimity and inclusivity, where we observe our thoughts, emotions, and external circumstances without becoming excessively attached or aversive to them. To fully embody we must cultivate a non-judgmental and accepting attitude toward whatever arises. We find refuge here as the mind stills. This tranquil state of existence grants crystal clear vision, thus empowering us to make choices that resonate with all of life. In embodying neutrality, we transform narrow egoic perspectives into expansive views free from shortsided attempts to "fix" something. This sacred ground ensures that our creations are not tainted by doubt or fear.

Neutrality is the essence of conscious presence. This state is far from a retreat into indifference or apathy, nor is it confined to times of formal meditation. Rather, neutrality is an actionable state—the embodiment of a heightened, quiet awareness that we can learn to integrate daily. This unattached state allows one to navigate life's inevitable ebb and flow with an elegant poise, liberated from the chains of judgment and predefined boundaries.

Enacting neutrality is the skillfull act of detaching from thoughts and external realities that hold energetic ties, which can steer our choices and thereby reinforce patterns in our bodies that we no longer wish to live. Resting in neutrality, we are better able to see negativity and illusions as such. Here we see the power of each moment. That each moment, depending on how we orient to it, carries the possibility to set us free and create new pathways.

To fully grasp this truth we must be dedicated to cultivating insight. We must also be willing to pause and sit in the potential discomfort of neutrality caused by witnessing a recurring pattern and not getting tangled by our habitual way of reacting. New and unknown is inherently edgy. Can we relate to this edge or discomfort from a neutral state of acceptance? If so, we can more easily listen to our inner knowing and make decisions that are aligned with our highest good and in service to all life.

Until practiced, neutrality remains a mere theory. We may even reject it for being "too new agey" or doubt its potency since it is rooted in renunciation. Paradoxically however, it is often the simple acts that have the greatest impact. That said, when caught in the throes of a fight-flight-freeze response or when overwhelmed by anxiety, the concept of neutrality may feel "impossible" to apply. Yet, the very beauty lies in the application.

Ideally we can practice entering neutrality in calmer moments when we are not highly activated or charged. We can often hold ourselves to unrealistic levels of perfection. In noticing this pattern, try to release these expectations and allow for the unavoidable messiness of the repatterning process. Most important is that our intentions are clear and our effort is consistent. From this place, we can train our bodies to lean into this new vibrational state—centered and non-reactive.

Remember, all patterns born from separation seek resolution for our evolution. As we step into the Unity paradigm, a cascade of emotions can arise as our previously held beliefs—rooted in separation—begin to fall apart, leaving us feeling unstable. Cultivating a vibration of neutrality can support us in navigating this unfamiliar territory, allowing us to witness our evolution without reacting or inhibiting the process out of fear of change.

That said, whatever emotion manifests in the body is valid and must be honored in order for it to be released. We must relearn how to help our emotions be in motion. See it. Feel it. Move it.

By embodying neutrality, we become the witness. There is no wrong way. Have patience, it takes practice to enter neutrality. Each time we set the intention to embody neutrality, it becomes a visceral felt sense. As the body forms the memory of neutrality, it becomes easier to return to each time.

As a pattern becomes ripe to resolve, pre-echos ripple out as energetic reverberations in our field. As a pattern builds there comes a moment when we have the opportunity to either resolve or repeat the pattern. This is why entering into the neutrality of love—taking pause—is vital in the process. In time, we learn

32

to sense pre-echos as they emerge, cueing us to enter into neutrality. Here we are able to choose how we wish to respond. Resolving every pattern requires action, although sometimes this entails the act of doing nothing. Regardless of how we resolve the pattern, there will be post echos of the patterns. These post echos lead us to believe the pattern is not resolved, they are just shadows of the pattern.

These post echos hold no power. We may feel grief and loss after resolving a pattern. The pull to restart the resolved pattern to regain the familiar is part of the post echo phenomenon. We currently exist within an intensified and polarized paradigm of opposing viewpoints.

When we speak of resolving patterns, it can be confusing and feel as though some patterns never fully resolve. However, we can be sure that separation patterns will be completely resolved in the coming months and years. The reason we can be certain of this is that these patterns will no longer be vibrationally sustained as the vibration of both the body and the Earth reaches a tipping point into Unity vibration. For now, we weaken these stubborn patterns as they reappear exponentially, giving us opportunities to resolve them. Every time we witness these familiar patterns in neutrality, it weakens them further until they are fully resolved. This polarization manifests as a gradual yet constant depletion of our personal and collective energy, often leaving us feeling angry, frustrated, diminished, or disempowered. The very pursuit and practice of neutrality can aid this, thereby creating more space for play, joy, creativity, and abundance.

Neutrality is a living meditation and represents the art of emotional intelligence. As the observer we learn to respond with empathy and compassion, thus bringing these qualities to the forefront of our interactions. In turn, this practice enriches our understanding of the intricacy of human relationships. We all wish to live in a nonjudgmental environment. We must

33

turn within to make change, for it is self-judgment that breeds external judgment. Fortunately however, in the neutrality of love judgment cannot exist. Here in neutrality, we can validate our true nature, our emotions, and other humans all while not feeding the wolf of separation.

Adverse reactions stem from a sense of separation. The imbalanced ego—in its quest for validation—often insists on being right and feeds off the surge of energy released by the endocrine system when defending the illusion of separation. The ego however, does not realize that these bursts of energy are not sustainable sources of vitality.

At the core of our being lives the neutrality of love, where all solutions exist free from separation. This is our Divinity. From this deep space, we begin to trust our internal guidance system and cultivate new origin seeds—patterns of Unity—within us.

From the vantage point of neutrality, we can embrace the belief that every facet of our experience is co-created in service to our evolution, which in turn facilitates our extraordinary human journey.

These advanced, yet simple teachings will bring those who are ready into the radical remembrance of Unity. From this place, a new purpose emerges as to why we are here. We become the bridge to Unity for others. It is a true honor and pleasure to be a catalyst for awaking. We are all in this together and no one is better than another. Concepts of hierarchy and comparison are unjust and based in the old separation paradigm. Those who remember first are simply the souls that are ready. Are the flowers who bloom first innately superior to their neighbors who are soon to unfurl their petals? Of course not. From this knowing, we may take action from the heart of neutrality.

The balanced integrated energy we emit is of far greater concern than the energy we receive, as we are the process of alchemy itself. Mastering the art of neutrality however is essential to fully unleash our alchemical potential. Awakening does not have to be a tedious slog, however does require steady effort. To refine our skills, we simply practice. In any scenario we can become the observer. Notice subtle shifts in our energy as we respond to stimuli while staying aligned with our true nature. Then celebrate the newfound enthusiasm and abundance born from living and acting in Unity.

Neutrality in all situations.

In our daily lives, we encounter numerous situations that challenge our ability to remain neutral and open-minded. The practice of neutrality, however, can be cultivated in every aspect of our lives, bringing a sense of calm and clarity to our interactions and experiences both inner and outer.

Let's begin with the simple act of lying down in bed at night. As we settle into the pillow, we can observe thoughts as they arise and pass through our minds. Without judgment or blame, we allow them to flow—like clouds drifting across the sky. We can turn awareness to the breath, sensing the effortless movement in and out, as our body relaxes into the mattress. This is the practice of acceptance—allowing whatever arises to arise, without resistance or attachment to the body or mind being a certain way.

When we wake, we can practice extending this state of being into the rest of our day. Before rising from bed, take a few moments to lay in neutrality—observing thoughts and sensations without judgment. The length of time can vary—20 seconds to 10 minutes—whatever feels accessible and intuitive. It is best to rely on our inner sense of timing, rather than looking at the clock to determine when to transition.

Throughout the day we can continue exploring neutrality. In the bathroom, while driving, at work, or in the grocery store, simply take a moment to pause and recenter ourselves observing present thoughts, feelings, and sensations without opinion. Try habit stacking, the pairing of mindful awareness with habitual doings such as brushing the teeth, washing hands, opening a door. In turn, we gradually weave the state of neutrality into our diverse and dynamic lives creating inner peace and safety.

By practicing neutrality in a variety of settings we do not become dependent on "perfect" external or internal circumstances. This is essential to be able to live in neutrality. Further, it is an embodiment of Unity for only entering neutrality in curated times, such as formal meditation, could be seen as a form of separation.

Once the body establishes a memory of neutrality, we can harness this state to make informed and intuitive decisions. Through this practice, we find a simple yet powerful way to navigate our human experience in both an inclusive and expansive manner—free from undue influence by fear. By allowing our inner knowing to grow in the fertile ground of neutrality, we empower ourselves. In attuning to the wisdom of our bodies, we gain access to a wealth of information and insights that may not be immediately apparent to the conscious mind.. As we become more attuned to our emotions and physical sensations, we are resourced to make choices in alignment with our true nature of Unity. Furthermore, by cultivating neutrality the body is granted the opportunity to rest, healing the nervous system. When we no longer feel the need to guard and defend our beliefs, we open ourselves to deeper listening and more thoughtful responses—ones that bring harmony rather than division. As our inner barriers soften, our energy expands, creating space for new possibilities to unfold. We begin to allow for greater flow in our lives. From this place of acceptance, we discover a deeper strength—one rooted in resilience and adaptability—allowing us to meet challenges with ease and grace.

Neutrality Meditation

This meditation invites you to actively surrender, fostering a state of neutrality. It's designed to establish an elemental pattern that serves as a foundation for creating unity elemental patterns.

Practice Schedule:
Days 1–3: Practice three times a day.
Days 4–9: Increase to six times a day.
Day 10 onward: Increase to nine times a day.
You can continue increasing in sets of three, adjusting to a frequency that feels right for you.

Meditation Steps:
Duration: Each session lasts less than 30 seconds.
Breathing: Take a deep breath in, releasing all thoughts as you exhale.
Surrender: If thoughts arise, gently let them ride on each out-breath.
Focus: Tune out external sounds, embracing even a momentary sense of neutrality. Achieving even a brief instant of neutrality establishes a new elemental pattern in Unity. To nurture and strengthen this pattern, consistent repetition is key. While each session is brief, totaling a minimum of 90 seconds daily, the emphasis is on quality over duration. Keeping sessions concise aids in maintaining vibrational continuity.

After mastering this practice, it can be utilized to manifest purpose. However, it's advisable to focus solely on the meditation for at least 21 days before integrating it into manifestation practices. Keep the process simple and practice in various settings to enhance adaptability.

Herbal Insights: Blue Vervain

Blue vervain (Verbena hastata), often called the "Enchanter's Herb," has been cherished across cultures for its medicinal and spiritual properties. Used by the ancient Egyptians, Greeks, Romans, and Celtic Druids, this revered plant continues to offer deep healing and connection today.

Ways to connect with Blue Vervain
☽ Tea & Tincture and can be smoked: Benefits & Energetic Properties
🌿 Harmony & Spiritual Well-Being – Encourages inner peace, love, and balance.
🌿 Enhancing Intuition & Dream Work – Traditionally used to deepen intuitive awareness and unlock inner wisdom.

CHAPTER FOUR

ELEMENTAL PATTERNS

TRUST ALL PATTERNS

At the moment of creation's spark, in a state of neutrality, elemental patterns emerge and set themselves in motion. We can picture them as spirals, turning upward and gradually tightening with each rotation. These patterns are designed to resolve when they reach a point where no further movement is possible. At that moment, a new spark ignites, giving rise to a fresh pattern infused with evolutionary information. In nature, there is no true end—only transformation. Every elemental pattern eventually resolves, giving birth to the next, continuing the flow of creation.

These patterns shape the reality we experience, weaving us into their structure. Whether vast or subtle, every pattern plays a role, interwoven with all others. These cycles create order in our daily lives, forming the very fabric of existence. Each pattern carries its own purpose, providing a steady foundation as we move through the simulation of life. Like projectors of light, they shape the physical world—without them, matter itself could not exist.

These elemental patterns follow the mathematical structure of 3D frequencies, which can be measured by equations like the Golden Ratio and the Fibonacci sequence. We see this pattern manifest in the Flower of Life and in platonic solids that create stable sacred geometry that the universe is created from. These structures hold The elemental patterns of nature manifest across all scales of existence, from the smallest particles to the largest cosmic structures. These patterns emerge as music, the spiral of a sunflower, the dynamics of relationships, the arrangement of cellular structures, and the organization of entire solar systems and galaxies. These invisible blueprints become tangible when they are expressed as elemental patterns—the fundamental shapes and forms that underlie the structure of the physical world.

Thus, we are not just beings of matter but projections of light, shaped by the elemental patterns that guide the formation of the universe itself. Everything in existence, from the smallest atom to the vastness of space, follows these same elemental principles, uniting all of creation in a shared fractal geometry.

From the moment of conception, we carry a unique Origin seed, containing the fundamental patterns that guide our growth from embryo to newborn. Within this seed are past life imprints, inherited family traits, Soul lineage, and the shared patterns of the human species. From these core blueprints, additional layers take form—our beliefs, biological rhythms, daily habits, thoughts, relationships, ancestral ties, addictions, and behaviors—all woven into the unfolding design of our personal elemental patterns.

Intellectual understanding can only take us so far—what truly matters is trusting the patterns that shape our experience. These patterns, through repetition, weave a vibrational continuity into the body, subtly influencing our perception and movement through life. Whether they arise from the illusion of separation or the reality of Unity, they continue to emerge, inviting us to recognize them. Each recurrence presents a choice: to resolve them and shift into new timelines or to remain within them, gathering deeper wisdom along the way. Every cycle brings us to a pivotal moment—a choice point. If we are aware of it, we can consciously decide: do we surrender to the unknown, embracing transformation, or do we stay in the familiar, allowing the pattern to repeat once more?

Summary

The spark of creation arises from the connection between masculine and feminine energies within the neutrality of love. From this union, an Origin seed is created, forming a crystalline structure. This structure is the beginning of an elemental pattern. The next step in the process of birthing an elemental pattern is this energy-information entering into Water birthing the pattern into the physical reality. Water is the catalyst for all life

Life is always modeling the elemental patterns woven throughout existence—the changing seasons, the rhythmic rise and fall of the sun, and the ebb and flow of the tides, which move in harmony with the lunar cycle. These larger Earth-based patterns don't just shape the external world; they influence our internal landscape as well. Our emotions, like the tides, are deeply connected to these natural cycles, and the waters within our bodies respond to their shifting rhythms. In a world that often feels chaotic, these steady, recurring patterns provide something to lean on, helping to ground our bodies as the reality we once knew begins to dissolve.

As we transition into a new paradigm, we can recognize it as an elemental pattern completing its cycle. The separation paradigm, too, is a pattern that has served its purpose, shaping our experience and teaching us in ways we are only beginning to understand. Now, a new pattern is emerging—the Unity paradigm. With this deeper awareness, we see that separation is no longer necessary; its role in our evolution has been fulfilled. As we attune to the greater resonant frequency of this global shift, we move toward a much higher vibration. In this process, all of our personal elemental patterns—once entangled in the illusion of separation—naturally begin to resolve, allowing us to step fully into a new resonant frequency-Unity

Every personal pattern we engage with creates vibrational continuity within the body, shaping the resonant frequency we carry. Put simply, the patterns we embody determine the overall vibration we hold. The same is true for the Earth itself. Just as our personal vibrational state is influenced by the patterns we embody, the Earth's energetic field is shaped by the collective frequencies it sustains.

We are now experiencing an exponential resolution of separation patterns in the body. The reason for this is the collective vibration is shifting due to the earth's overall vibration shifting into the Unity paradigm.

Even though we may wish to control when these patterns resolve, their unfolding is inevitable. Fortunately, the divine orchestration of this shift follows a compassionate and caring design.

Those who are ready—whose souls have arrived at the moment of releasing the patterns of separation—will be the first to move through this transformation. This is part of their soul's journey, a sacred contract that calls them to resolve and evolve these patterns before others. In doing so, they establish a new personal paradigm, one that aligns with a higher vibrational field of elemental patterns and beliefs. Their transformation is not only for themselves—it is an act of service, a way to illuminate the path so that others may follow when they, too, are ready.

These deeply ingrained patterns are woven into our daily lives, making them challenging to resolve. At times, it may feel as if we are losing control. The familiarity and sense of security they once provided no longer hold in the same way. As they begin to implode, we may experience a cascade of emotions, and on the other side, a new internal and external reality reveals itself more swiftly than we expect. While it may seem like we are surrendering free will, this is merely an illusion. In truth, we are evolving toward a more expansive and authentic expression of it.

The challenge lies in allowing these patterns to resolve without resistance. It is through resistance that we experience heightened chaos and disruptive energetic nodes—slowing the process but never stopping it. No matter what we do, the shift into Unity remains inevitable.

As larger Earth patterns shift alongside significant astrological events, we are given a unique window of time—a portal through which separation patterns can dissolve effortlessly, making space for new patterns rooted in Unity to emerge. This moment invites us to release what has kept us bound to separation and align with the evolving rhythms of Unity.

Our task is not to force these changes but to gently allow them. The action we take is one of surrender—letting jobs, routines, and habitual negative thought patterns shift as they are meant to. Of course, this is not always easy.

Free will is more than just choice—it is the ongoing dance of creation and resolution. Every moment, we are shaping, resolving, and creating new elemental patterns, whether through thought, action, or intention. Life itself is a continuous interplay of these patterns, expanding and resolving in cycles that guide our evolution. Rather than a static force, free will is fluid—woven into the very fabric of existence. Each decision, whether conscious or unconscious, participates in this ever-unfolding process. The more we align with the natural rhythm of resolution and expansion, the more gracefully we navigate life's unfolding design. In this way, free will is not simply about control, but about co-creating with the unseen forces that shape our reality.

The speed at which the separation pattern resolves depends on how long it has been active. If active for a few months it may fade quickly. After 40 years of being continually reinforced it will undoubtedly take more time, but resolution is still possible. As the pattern resolves, there will be an increased flow of energy in the body and the individual's overall vibration will rise.

In grasping the Origins of and reasons behind our patterns, we begin to view them differently. We can realize that these patterns are not inherently bad—that they initially arose to protect us and that they are designed to be healed, to resolve, so we can evolve.

Though it may not always be obvious, all patterns are rooted in love, as the universe itself is created from the neutrality of love. Every cycle, no matter how chaotic it may seem, ultimately serves the purpose of evolution and alignment.

Repetition plays a profound role in this process, establishing vibrational continuity. Where and how we place our attention directly impacts the unfolding of patterns—determining whether they resolve with ease or remain stagnant in the birthing process. Awareness of this dynamic allows us to become active participants in the transformation of our reality.

Deepening our relationship with each element is how we quicken this process with ease. Through the cultivation of elemental practices, we exponentially resolve any separation patterns that keep us from believing we are innately the elements. They are alive and are inviting us to engage with them through these practices.

Mastering the ability to enter neutrality is also key to allowing Unity patterns to take shape. In neutrality, we become conduits for new patterns to emerge, free from the interference of resistance or attachment. This is where true co-creation begins.

Water

Life begins in Water. Without it, life would not exist. Water is the neutrality of love. All patterns are born into the tangible, physical realm through the element of Water. Water is the essence of motherly love. In the womb, she insulates the Origin Seed—the fetus—keeping them safe as they begin to grow. Water is where the manifestation process takes root—it is through Water's benevolence that life is supported and created.

From a neutral and receptive state, Water witnesses reality objectively, free of illusions. Acting as a constant mirror, she clearly reflects reality. Whatever vibration we emit, Water emulates. Understanding the neutrality of Water is essential to fully fathom that we—all life—are vibrational sponges. Like a mother, Water intends to nourish and support growth while simultaneously granting us freedom to be spiritually sovereign.

Water plays a vital role in storing and transmitting information within living organisms. On a cellular level, water serves as a fundamental medium for exchanging and processing information. She ensures the seamless flow of nutrients, removal of waste, and communication between molecules—all of which is essential for proper cellular function and maintaining homeostasis.

Moreover, Water's unique properties allow the element to act as a conduit, transferring information throughout entire biological systems. Our bodies' intricate network of blood vessels and lymphatic channels are primarily composed of water. This aqueous network enables the transportation of hormones, immune cells, and other regulatory factors, thus ensuring proper communication and coordination between distant organs and tissues.

The fluidity of our joints is another testament to Water's vital role in the body. The synovial fluid that lubricates our joints contains a complex mixture of proteins, lipids, and other molecules that offer cushioning between bones and cartilage, thus reducing friction. This fluid allows for smooth joint movement, enabling us to perform a wide range of physical activities with ease.

Water brilliantly forms hydrogen bonds, making it ideal for storing and transmitting information. Hydrogen bonds are intermolecular forces that allow Water molecules to form transient networks between one another and with other molecules. These molecular networks store and transmit information through vibrational patterns, similar to electrical signals that pass information through electronic circuits.

Given Water's dynamic wisdom, she carries the key to our collective paradigm shift. While Fire (solar heat) and Earth send ascension waves with vibrational upgrades, it is the liquid element that transfers energetic codes into the body by activating dormant DNA that are surrounded by Water molecules. Without the element of Water, it would be impossible to fully embody Unity.

Water plays a primary role in creating and establishing elemental patterns. However, as the Unity paradigm emerges and new elemental patterns form, the vibration of Water living on Earth and within us will reset.

This transformation clears all lingering patterns of separation, allowing only Unity patterns to remain.

This phenomenon can also be explained through cymatics, the study of visible sound and vibration, and how sound frequencies impact physical form. Given that the molecular structure of Water stores information, the element embodies all surrounding frequencies. In the context of sacred geometry, Water is a matrix containing all patterns associated with a particular dimension. Sacred geometries, such as the Flower of Life or Metatron's Cube, are a representation of the vibrational energy held within Water.

Water is a natural force of renewal, capable of resetting our energy flows. A daily conscious connection with water—whether through touch, movement, or intention—can bring profound shifts. Even a simple splash of fresh water on our face can invigorate and realign our energy, while a quick cold shower can instantly shift a pattern. We can also connect by acknowledging the water we drink, infusing it with gratitude and love before it nourishes us.

How do you connect with water?

Can you find a way to engage with her each day?

We are always in communication with the water within our bodies. When we create new patterns that honor this awareness, we support the body's natural state of homeostasis. By recognizing and respecting water both inside and around us, we deepen our connection to Unity.

Wind

Wind—an eternal exchange between the outer and inner air—a connector of life. When we breathe with awareness, the potency of the breath transforms. Taking just a few minutes each hour to follow the breath in and out with presence directly influences the flow of energy in the body. As we do this, the biological metaphysics of the body shifts. Every breath marks the beginning and end of an elemental pattern. We are offered the opportunity to resolve patterns that are ripe and ready for change with each breath, in every moment. Fueled by the movement of fire, wind contains water, moving across and within the earth element. Each time we breathe. With each breath, a similar process unfolds. We can witness the connections and elemental patterns of life through the simple act of breathing. It is a continuous exchange of reciprocity—giving and receiving. Yet, most of us move through life unaware of how we breathe or the sacredness held within each inhale and exhale.

In time, we will remember that our breath carries the power to resolve patterns that are ready to heal. By breathing in feelings of love and gratitude and allowing these Unity frequencies to flow outward with each exhale, we can direct healing to any part of the body that holds pain or trauma. Soon, we will come to see that many ailments can be transformed through elemental practices.

Wind is a felt element, alive in the unseen. It reminds us that not everything that exists can be seen, teaching us to trust in what lies beyond sight. Though the majority of our reality is unseen, our culture often places greater value on what can be seen and touched.

By learning to honor the unseen—the nature of connection, the wisdom within—we begin to trust our inner knowing, free from doubt and shame. Wind becomes a guide, a catalyst that invites us to step into the inner world that patiently awaits our arrival.

Cultivating a relationship with wind is effortless, like a Sunday morning. It is as simple as calling it forth with an invitation of any kind—a drumbeat, a song, a movement. Air is ever present. Even on the calmest of days a breeze will come and caress our face, reminding us of the vast and powerful energies swirling around us at all times.

Wind is a channel, a conduit facilitating the movement and vitality of both water and fire. In the absence of wind, water and fire would fall stagnant—lifeless.

Fire

We witness potent and powerful changes with the fire element. Created by friction, fire is the embodiment of movement—of transformation. The heat of fire is absolute. There is no space to doubt or question once fire is ignited.

Our inner fire is always present, quietly waiting for the right conditions to ignite and burn with purpose. By deepening our relationship with the elements, we refine our ability to sense our own natural rhythms. With this awareness, we can recognize when to stoke our fire, channeling its energy with intention and clarity.

Fire ignites our will, infusing us with the courage to venture into the unknown. When we have had enough; when the status quo can no longer be tolerated and we must resolve a habitual separation pattern; when we are ready to alchemize our purpose into action, the invitation is to get angry! Anger can be supportive of resolving a stubborn pattern or simply stoking the fire of passion within. It is a vital element to create tangible change in our lives. Fire is the embodiment of change, the only element that can alchemise another element.

Holding onto anger is toxic. If suppressed, it will find a way to emerge in explosive ways, burning everything in its path causing more harm than good. As a seed needs just the right amount of heat to sprout, small increments of anger paired with intention can be a catalyst for positive change—for the greater good. We will learn to cultivate this skill.

We invite fire to burn it all away—synergizing anger with a loving surrender. Let it all go! Most likely we will quickly realize the illusionary patterns we cling to don't stand a chance with fire's power. The phoenix rises from the ashes. A new pattern is born!

It is through the merging of water and air that we are able to maintain the ideal temperature for our inner fire. Excessive wind, water, or earth can extinguish the fire—halting all powers of manifestation. Likewise, too hot a fire will burn the seeds of creation.

Remembering the Unity of the elements—within us and beyond—we learn to activate their powers to guide us in navigating ascension upgrades with grace.

Herb for fire element: Cinnamon, Cayenne Pepper, and Ginger

Add these spices generously to your cooking to stimulate your digestive fire--your agni.

Earth

The Earth nurtures and sustains all life with her boundless and unconditional love, providing us with the essential foundation for growth. Without her vessel, our physical existence would be impossible.

Her embrace is exemplified by the way she cradles rivers with her banks, anchoring trees in the ground. Earth creates a harmonious environment for life to thrive without undue chaos.

The physical boundaries of the Earth, namely the atmosphere and gravity, protect us from burning to ash or floating into the ethers. She shields us from solar radiation and meteoroids, anchoring us into the ground. These boundaries, while protective, do not create a closed ecosystem. Energy constantly flows in and out of this dynamic system. The universal truth of movement and exchange, emphasize the significance of energy balance. The flow of energy into and out of the system must be proportional to maintain equilibrium.

The Earth and her ecosystem are constantly evolving and growing. It is through this universal exchange that everything is in constant movement. As Earth's natural algorithms in the toroidal field are reset, greater balance will be restored preventing mass extinction.

In our individual lives, the Earth element embodies the resolution of our elemental patterns. This element is the ground where relationships solidify, forming long-lasting friendships and intimate partnerships. Earth is home to all physical manifestations where seeds and ideas blowing in the breath of Wind find ground—where projects, businesses, and collaborations flourish. This is not the end of a cycle, but rather the beginning of an upward spiral, signifying the never-ending pattern that gains momentum by rooting into Earth.

The Earth is our body. We are animated Earth. With Water and Wind moving through and creating our shape, our bodies are like planet Earth—a vessel to all. Like Mother Earth, Fire burns within our bodies, warming us from the core. Fire burns in physical processes such as digestion as well as in emotional and spiritual alchemy.

There is immense power in honoring and remembering the elements that live within us—are us. In turn, a sweet and genuine sense of belonging emerges as the search for identity fades and we consciously embody our place. This is the essence of Unity, we are not separate from the elements. Rather, we are one with them.

Herbal Insights: Licorice & Ginseng
Both of these adaptogens help move stagnant energy, making them powerful allies for elemental practices.

Ways to Connect with Licorice & Ginseng
☽ **Tea, Tincture & Powder** – The most common methods for internal use, allowing their healing properties to integrate with the body.

Energetic Benefits
🌿 **Licorice Root** (*Glycyrrhiza glabra*) – Supports adrenal health, clears the lungs, and soothes inflammation. A deep breath with licorice helps restore balance.
🌿 **Ginseng** (*Panax spp.*) – Boosts energy, sharpens focus, and enhances vitality. A trusted root for strength and endurance.

\

The creaking and groaning of stagnant waters echo through the cavernous crevices of ingrained patterns, shifting ever so slowly. With each subtle movement, the earth begins to open, clearing away what was once broken. In its wake, it leaves the spirit of grief and sadness—the very threshold to joy, the gateway to expansive openness. This unfolding invites us to trust, to surrender, as the once-still waters transform into the rushing rapids of life, carrying us forward into the unknown with renewed flow.

CHAPTER FIVE

BELIEFS

*EVERY BELIEF HAS A UNIQUE VIBRATIONAL SIGNATURE.
COMBINED, THESE BELIEFS CREATE THE
UNIFIED VIBRATION OF THE BODY*

Given that Unity beliefs already exist within us, the last thing we need is someone telling us what to believe. However, being invited to turn toward the wisdom and Unity that dwells within us can support awakening this part of ourselves. The intention of this book is to inspire the integration of Unity beliefs through our inner knowing. So, let's spread our wings and rise together into our spiritual sovereignty, supported by the foundational belief that all life is interconnected, created from love, innately safe, and that the possibilities ahead are limitless.

Living in abundance or scarcity is directly shaped by what we believe to be true or possible. The strength of each belief depends on the energy we give it. Within the body, countless beliefs are stored, forming intricate structures that influence the entire system.

Each belief carries a vibrational signature, emitting a specific frequency that contributes to the body's overall vibration. This is how our energetic state is formed. Shifting these beliefs—and the patterns they create within the body—is a vital part of the paradigm shift we are stepping into.

First, we must clarify definitions. Then, we can enact change.

Belief: A belief is a mental attitude where an individual accepts something to be true or real. A variety of influences can inspire beliefs such as family lineage, personal experiences, religious, cultural and societal influences, scientific discoveries and philosophical theories. Beliefs are not always backed by facts or empirical evidence. Rather, they are held as truths within an individual and their unique perception of reality. Beliefs shape an individual from their thoughts and actions, to relationships, synchronicities, and timelines, to their abundance or scarcity. Each belief plays a role in crafting the overall vibration of the body and ripples out, influencing and co-creating the collective consciousness.

Limiting Separation Beliefs: Such beliefs stem from a contracted state, diminishing our trust in both ourselves and others. They slow the evolutionary process and restrict the natural flow of life force within the body. Separation-based or limiting beliefs are often rigid and absolute, reinforcing an illusion of division and scarcity. They filter reality through the lens of the known, leaving little room for the emergence of new possibilities and untapped potentials. Often rooted in religious or scientific dogma, these beliefs dismiss inner knowing and disconnect us from the living wisdom of the natural world.

Their persistence is fueled by personal fears and reinforced through pervasive fear-based narratives. Separation-based beliefs masquerade as protective mechanisms for survival, yet in reality, they obstruct healing and contribute to dis-ease. They foster apathy, complacency, and stagnation, disrupting balance and increasing entropy. The consequences of these patterns are evident in countless ways—from the degradation of our ecosystems to the widespread strain on individual nervous systems.

Separation beliefs must be defended and thus create division, leading to violence, wars, & dis-ease.

Unity-Based Beliefs: A Unity-based belief is rooted in connection and love, fostering compassion, understanding, empathy, and a sense of purpose. These beliefs are expansive, open to growth and change, and naturally inclusive. They encourage personal sovereignty, greater free will, and abundance for all.

The vibration of Unity beliefs resonates with our true nature, harmonizing masculine and feminine energies and opening energetic pathways within the body's biofield. This allows vital information to flow more freely, supporting healing, strengthening intuition, enhancing neuroplasticity, and deepening trust in ourselves and others.

This dynamic mirrors the balance found in Earth's ecosystems and within the micro-ecosystems of our bodies. As entropy decreases, regeneration takes hold, and new solutions naturally emerge.

Unity beliefs never need to be defended.

We need beliefs to navigate, function, and survive. They provide purpose and an energetic structure to organize around. While not all of our beliefs are rooted in separation, the vibration of the separation paradigm creates a baseline that many of our beliefs stem from. These separation filters appear in our daily language, pop-culture media, religions and politics as subtle yet potent innuendos that ultimately diminish our sense of inner Divinity.

For instance, we invest significant time and energy into a project until it is ready to be shared with the world. We have strong faith that our offering will help others, yet just before the release, subtle doubts begin to creep in. Seeking reassurance, we may confide in our community. While they may support our efforts, they might also highlight potential risks that could jeopardize the project, perhaps in an attempt to protect us—or even with subtler motives like jealousy woven into their words. Much of this advice stems from the separation beliefs they hold within. Even when the advice is wrapped in positive reinforcement, these separation filters pepper it with doubts and apprehension, which resonate with the separation beliefs within us. This activates our fear of the unknown and may even resurface past failures, stretching back to childhood. Over time, we begin to recognize this pattern of so-called "protection" as an illusion of separation, reflected in our beliefs, childhood experiences, conversations, and actions. For this reason, it's important to keep those newly germinated seeds of creation grounded in Unity to ourselves until they gather momentum.

All separation beliefs are created as elemental patterns and thus seek resolution and on the other hand Unity beliefs seek expansion as no belief is intended to be stagnant. When separation beliefs feel limiting it is often because they are fixed and unchanging, directly opposing the energy of growth. However, whether these beliefs are rooted in separation or Unity they play a vital role in our evolution. While it may seem easy to label them as "good" or "bad," this is an illusion of separation that further amplifies polarity. When we acknowledge that everything is vibrational, the polarizing effect of limiting beliefs will diminish.

Separation Belief
"Limiting beliefs are bad."

The overall vibration we embody is our resonant frequency. To maintain a steady Unity vibration and raise the body's resonant frequency, we must reconstruct our belief system from the ground up. This begins with fully embracing Unity beliefs, allowing separation belief patterns to resolve.

When we direct our attention toward separation beliefs, we unintentionally feed them, strengthening their hold within our system. Without realizing it, we reinforce their influence simply by focusing on them.

Outdated separation beliefs do not resonate with our true nature; they rely on a constant stream of low vibrations rooted in fear to stay relevant. As the Unity paradigm strengthens—both globally and within us—the continuous rise in vibration will begin to dissolve separation belief patterns, both collectively and individually. During this transition, we will witness a surge of negativity, fear of the unknown, and a growing fear within ourselves. As the belief structures we have grown accustomed to shift, this fear is being purged, becoming more visible and deeply felt. This marks the separation paradigm's final attempt to maintain its illusion of power—a last gasp. Despite these exaggerated efforts, the rise of Unity is inevitable. It's important to understand that we are not separate from this illusion.

By actively beginning the process of embodying Unity beliefs, we create a container for a Unity belief system to take root and grow. As we resolve fundamental separation beliefs, we minimize the shock to the body as the illusion of separation collapses from within. Separation beliefs have a strong grip on our nervous system and neurological pathways, and when fed by our attention, they can trigger the release of chemical compounds that spark emotional responses. If a core separation belief is resolved too quickly, without Unity beliefs in place to cushion the impact, we may experience a jarring and unpleasant "death cycle." Additionally, since beliefs serve as our internal navigation system, it's helpful to have a new belief structure simultaneously rising to guide us once the old paradigm begins to be dismantled Within us.

This highlights the importance of incremental upgrades and being a conscious supporter of our evolution, rather than the forceful driver. Allowing separation beliefs to resolve in their own timing creates space for Unity beliefs to simultaneously emerge, creating a new foundation for us to stand upon.

Rest assured, nature has devised a precise plan for our collective awakening. There will come a time when millions, and eventually billions, of humans will be ready to embody the divinity of Unity. We will each blossom when the conditions are just right.

Unity Belief
"I trust we will all awaken in divine timing."

The vast majority of us will experience incremental vibrational shifts. The process of constructing a Unity belief structure is an intimate and unique personal journey. Regardless of what we do or who we are, all separation belief structures will be dismantled creating space for the Unity belief structure to emerge. The vast cosmic nature of this vibrational shift assures us it will happen to everyone in due time. Earth's frequency continually rises as the Unity paradigm emerges from within the planet's toroidal field as well as from within the biofield of individual life forms.

The scientific explanation for this transformation is rooted in the laws of resonance. The integration of Unity is a complex, dynamic process involving several principles: resonance, entrainment, interference, energy exchange, and harmonic blending. Resonance refers to the natural tendency of systems to vibrate at the same frequency when they are in harmony with one another. Entrainment occurs when a stronger frequency trains a weaker frequency into alignment with the influencing force, which can cause the emergence of synchronicities. Interference is experienced when waves interact—either amplifying one another or canceling the other out. Through energy exchange, systems share vibrational frequencies, thus influencing each other's state. Lastly, harmonic blending ensures that vibrations merge smoothly to create a new, unified frequency honoring and embodying elements from both paradigms. As the Heart and mind align with the unified vibration, we begin to experience a more cohesive state of being. The blending of these frequencies reflect the natural progression toward a more interconnected way of existing.

To enhance our conscious participation and infuse the journey with a sense of adventure, we can actively support the embodiment of Unity beliefs. By embracing these beliefs, speaking them aloud, holding them in our thoughts and heart, and visualizing their truth taking root, we eventually unveil the blueprint of our soul's Unity purpose.

As Unity beliefs ascend and the flow of vital energy increases, a creative spark is ignited to guide our path. This process unlocks Fifth-dimensional (5-D) frequencies at the cellular level, activating dormant crystalline structures in our DNA. In this state, we consciously reconnect with all life through our bodies, the quantum field, fellow human kin, and the natural world at large. Unlike computers, we possess the unique ability to make decisions inspired by the flow of Divinity—transcending conventional norms.

We begin where we are. We do not need permission from an external source to launch us. All we need is the willingness to begin where we are. Although such attributes may feel desirable, we do not need to be spiritually enlightened, monetarily wealthy, or have a fit body to evolve. With Unity beliefs at the helm, we may be surprised by what we are capable of.

Unity Belief
"I begin where I am."

Free of judgment about past decisions All of those indiscretions were created from separation, a scarcity mindset. deep wounding, and programming.

While we are responsible for our decisions and actions, ideally we do not feel unduly saddled by their weight. We free ourselves from the confines of judgment when we recognize how our past actions were influenced by separation and unresolved patterns. The moment we release regret and shame we embody Unity. To further establish this newfound state, we can take action to forgive and make amends to ourselves and others.

Unity Belief
"I am worthy of enlightenment!"

The resolution of a separation belief can be equated to part of us dying. We have invested significant energy into our limiting beliefs and are accustomed to defending them. Hence we must move through stages of denial, bargaining, anger, and sadness before we can rest in acceptance. As mentioned previously, having select Unity belief structures already present ensures the death process is as easeful as possible.

Unity Belief
"In every decision, I choose love over fear."

Fundamental beliefs create the foundation of the belief system we embody. Both paradigms, be it separation or Unity, are founded upon fundamental beliefs.

* Fundamental belief of the separation paradigm
"I am not safe."

This fundamental belief is the source of all other separation beliefs. Once we resolve this illusion, all related beliefs begin to unravel. The notion of safety, or lack thereof, serves as a strong vibrational anchor as it is connected to our root chakra and elicits the body's instinctual, animalistic responses. With all separation beliefs arising from this core pattern, it requires a significant overhaul to release the survival mechanism of the limbic system or "lizard brain" and realign with our Divine nature and the truth that we are generally safe. Given the deep and ancient roots of this pattern, have patience as it will take intention, time, and effort to release the fear belief.

The sympathetic nervous system ("fight-flight-freeze") is a brilliantly designed mechanism to defend against predators. However, our overly stimulating culture exploits this part of our being, keeping our systems on high alert, never resting into the regenerative parasympathetic nervous system ("rest and digest"). The sympathetic response was never intended to be a constant state, rather one that awoke in times of great need. Overuse of this system creates neurological loops, leading to habitual fear-based thinking. Staying caught in the sympathetic state or the limbic loop is how the veil of illusion first came to be. When the flow of energy in the body slows down, stagnation forms as there is decreased energy circulating in the body. In turn, scarcity beliefs are made manifest and our evolution is stalled.

To truly understand what is unfolding, we are invited to embody a neutral perspective. Since our beliefs shape our reality, the deep-seated belief that *I am not safe* manifests both individual and collective experiences where safety feels compromised. This belief fuels control mechanisms, violence, wars, and the idea that we need a government to protect us.

At its core, this is the illusion—we do not need a protector to keep us safe from ourselves. Recognizing this takes great self-awareness and courage, as we are often the ones unknowingly sustaining this fundamental belief.

* Foundational Unity Belief
"I am safe!"

Our true nature is expansive, loving, creative, intelligent, sexual, compassionate, curious, intuitive, abundant, vulnerable, trusting, honest, enthusiastic, powerful, passionate, and peaceful. This is a fundamental Unity belief. We often diminish these truths and excuse harmful behavior under the guise of separation and unjustly claim human nature is less than Divine.

Separation Belief:
"It's just human nature."

When embodying fundamental Unity beliefs, there is no need to defend them, as they are surrounded by a deep and unwavering truth. Unity beliefs can be expressed in an inclusive and expansive way, rooted in the neutrality of love. Through this, we begin to co-create a new way of relating to and using language.

Even when we disagree with someone's perspective, we can choose to honor their experience rather than impose our own beliefs—unless, of course, our goal is to spark debate or conflict. Likewise, when we judge or blame others for their beliefs, we unintentionally reinforce the very patterns of separation we seek to dissolve. Instead, we are invited to hold space for differences, allowing Unity to guide our interactions.

Unity Belief
"We are intimately connected to one another. We are mirrors reflecting our innate Divinity back to each other."

Unity beliefs encourage us to live authentically and vulnerablely. This may not always feel easy or even positive. We cannot bypass the ugliness of the separation paradigm. In turn, we must become the witness—resting in the neutrality of love—as we move through the death and transformation process.

Unity Belief
"Feeling it is healing it."

It is natural to doubt and feel uncomfortable while shedding our old, known ways. That said, we can better navigate the waves of ascension by learning ascension skills that support us as accompanying symptoms arise.

These symptoms can manifest as anxiety, digestive discomfort, fear of the unknown, sadness, heightened emotional triggers, self-judgment, external judgment, questioning one's sanity, as well as shifts in jobs, romantic relationships, friendships, or living situations. Fortunately however, these symptoms tend to be temporary. Waiting on the other side lies a new way of being—where the sun shines, the birds sing, and we feel a renewed sense of purpose to explore.

Here are a few suggestions to regulate such symptoms:

- Enter into the neutrality of love
- Cultivate purpose
- Breathe in gratitude and appreciation
- Create healing vibrations like vowel sounds or humming
- Leap into the unknown
- Move the body in whatever way feels good—whether it's stretching, yoga, walking, hiking, Tai chi, or dancing
- Connect with nourishing community
- Spend time in nature
- Explore your sexuality through self-touch and intimacy with others
- Rest and retreat
- Walk barefoot to ground
- Refresh with water, be it a shower or river dip
- Connect with plants and herbal allies
- Share time with other animals

Take it easy...Give yourself permission to simply be in the struggle for a while. The emotional pain you feel is real, but try not to fully succumb to it or accept it as absolute truth. All separation is an illusion—the body just doesn't know that yet. External separation beliefs have been deeply internalized, making them feel real, even when they are not.

Unity Belief
"I am powerful in my most vulnerable moments."

While it's natural to want to blame external structures for programming separation into us, doing so only deepens the divide. Instead, we can turn inward, sit with our hearts, and remember the love that resides within us. In this space, our attachment to separation begins to gently dissolve.

Unity Belief
"I am comfortable with being uncomfortable."

Every time we resolve a separation belief, we take an evolutionary leap. This creates a temporary vibrational void in the body—a fragile period where we may feel ungrounded and chaotic as the energetic ties connected to our emotional body begin to unravel. The length of this void depends on the intensity of the belief being resolved. Clearing a foundational belief that influenced many other beliefs will create a domino effect, resolving multiple separation beliefs at once. This creates a significant vibrational leap. Therefore, the process may feel emotionally un-manageable. However, if we have already been integrating Unity beliefs, the transition out of the void will be smoother and faster. On the other side of the void, we embody the vibrational upgrade and experience a newfound space for new Unity beliefs to emerge.

As we move beyond intellectualizing Unity beliefs and begin to embody them, our vibrational frequency lightens and we become more focused. Our emotional body stabilizes at a higher resonant frequency and the rebuilding of trust creates a stronger inner knowing. Each time we undergo this process the body learns how to adapt to these shifts, making the next transition easier. In doing so, we are not only reprogramming our own genetic codes but also influencing our family lineage as well as the collective. While some individuals may feel they have already awakened due to an awakening moment, the process will not be complete until everyone evolves. This is the essence of Unity—All is One.

This transformative process mirrors neuroplasticity, where the brain forms new neural connections while dissolving old ones as new experiences and beliefs take root. As we release limiting separation beliefs, outdated neural pathways weaken, allowing new, empowering pathways to emerge—supporting our shift into higher vibrational states.

This process also aligns with epigenetics, which demonstrates how our environment and mindset influence gene expression. Resolving separation beliefs not only transforms our present experience but can also shift our genetic expression, creating ripples that may impact future generations.

As the body's vibration rises, our external world begins to shift. We cultivate abundance and may feel a renewed sense of hope—not just for ourselves, but for the collective human experience.

Our inner knowing—our intuition—awakens, reminding us that we can trust. Trust that we are safe. Trust in our Divinity. Trust in each other. Trust in love. However, expanding our capacity for trust does not mean abandoning discernment. As the barriers dissolve, we remember our role as co-creators and step into the free will of authenticity.

Unity Belief
"We have reached the tipping point."

Transitional Beliefs

Transitional belief patterns arise when we have resolved many separation beliefs, but haven't yet embraced enough Unity beliefs for Unity to become our dominant inner paradigm. At this stage, we may feel that something is amiss. As the illusion of separation begins to lift, we may still hold strong to certain old beliefs. During this stage of evolution, people can succumb to conspiracy theories that further rigidity and separation, expending energy in the form of blame and judgment. This can cause people to question institutions such as the government, organized religion, the education system, and healthcare. The questioning of these institutions helps to rapidly change them . The danger is spending valuable energy pointing fingers instead of allowing solutions in Unity to come to the forefront. If we spend all our time and energy in conspiracy theories we feed energy into the 4th dimension. These actions lack personal accountability and sustain a victim mentality,

Transitional Belief:
"It is not my fault nor my responsibility.
It is their fault and thus their responsibility."

Unity Belief

I accept responsibility for contributing to the separation paradigm through certain beliefs and actions. I take responsibility for my individual awakening and for the collective's evolution—for I am part of the collective."

Transitional beliefs drain energy from the body. It's not that conspiracy theories lack truth or that there's no one to blame. Rather, dwelling on these ideas doesn't support the flourishing of our personal energy. When we shift our focus toward listening to our intuition and cultivating trust in our inner knowing, we begin to realize that Unity beliefs are rising from within. This new belief system we are embodying no longer seeks external validation, nor do we feel the need to defend ourselves. Unity is a powerful vibration, and it will always prevail!

Unity Practice

Each morning, whether out loud or in your mind, repeat the simple Unity affirmation: "I am safe, I am safe, I am safe."

Envision yourself feeling safe in various situations, particularly those that trigger discomfort or challenge. Even when we feel
uneasy, can we trust that we are safe? As you move through your day, practice this affirmation in different scenarios.

The body listens and responds to our intentions and actions, repatterning itself by forming new crystalline structures rooted in foundational Unity beliefs. Remember, by believing we are safe, we create a reality that reflects and radiates that safety.

Herbal Insights Yarrow & Cedar

Both of these plant allies offer protection and connection, serving as guides in both the seen and unseen realms.

Ways to Connect with Yarrow & Cedar

☽ **Yarrow** – Enjoy as a tea, tincture, or hang above the bed for protection and insight.

☽ **Cedar** – Use as an essential oil or smudge to purify and uplift sacred spaces.

Energetic Benefits

🌿 **Yarrow** *(Achillea millefolium)* – Known for amplifying psychic awareness and enhancing divination, yarrow acts as a bridge between the physical and spiritual realms. Drinking yarrow tea before sleep, paired with an intention for insight, may deepen dream experiences and intuitive guidance.

🌿 **Cedar** *(Cedrus spp.)* – A powerful protector, cedar dissolves the illusion of separation, revealing unity and connection. Its grounding presence clears fear and invites clarity, making it a sacred companion in spiritual practices.

CHAPTER SIX

ABUNDANCE

EMBRACING ABUNDANCE-
UNLOCKING UNITY

Abundance: a large quantity, or more than enough of something.

How about more than enough of everything? Is it possible to live a life where we have more than enough of everything? If we did, would it be acceptable? Given the current culture it is sadly hard to imagine all humans on Earth having more than enough. Is it possible to live on a planet where ecosystems are thriving? Where animals have healthy habitats and the Air and Water are clean?

As we begin to imagine a world that is abundant and safe it begins to manifest a world that is just that—safe and abundant. The key is to imagine it for everyone, not just for ourselves. The Origin seeds of abundance emerge once we are no longer saddled with contrary beliefs.

The scarcity mindset arises from separation beliefs and is rooted in the idea that resources, opportunities, and success are limited. Most of us, in one way or another, carry this mindset. For instance, rather than celebrating a friend's success we may fall into jealousy or believe there is now less for us. These beliefs generate fear, competition, and hoarding causing us to fixate on lack instead of abundance. It also creates anxiety, thus restricting our ability to take risks, share, or embrace opportunities for we are consumed by the fear of "not having enough." We are part of nature, which is inherently abundant. However, as we forget our true nature and adopt narrow mindsets we not only harm ourselves, but also fuel the destruction of Earth's ecosystem. The scarcity mindset is foundational to the illusion of separation paradigm, for it perpetuates the false belief that there is not enough to go around. In truth, there is more than enough for all of us—there is an abundance.

*Fundamental Separation Belief
"There isn't enough for everyone."

Unity Belief
"There is more than enough for everyone."

Our current economy is founded upon scarcity—skewed for a few to be unjustly wealthy, while the masses barely get by. Many workers are not paid a living wage (certainly not a thriving wage) and are expected to work overtime, all for the gain for those living on top of their gold towers. Tragically, many of us are caught in this survival work trap with few free hours to spend with loved ones, stoke our creative fires, and nourish ourselves.

The money we make vanishes to external expenses—taxes, car loans, mortgages, phone bills, utilities, food, and if we are lucky, savings. If we manage to balance this dance, our society deems it a good life. But that is a narrow, scarce notion of what life can be. These systems were not created from—or for—abundance, which is why they are not sustainable and soon will fall.

This isn't about adopting a different government or economic model. The real question is: *Shouldn't we all have more than enough?* The answer is yes. And it begins within us.

If we continue following the rules we've been taught, true abundance will remain out of reach. Desire and scarcity are the antithesis of abundance—like oil and water, they do not mix. Until we align with *Abundance-Unity-Love*, we remain out of vibrational attunement, stuck in scarcity, unable to open to the vast possibilities before us.

When we think of abundance, our minds often turn to money and survival. However, wealth alone does not equate to true abundance. Many wealthy individuals, including billionaires in the top 1%, still carry deeply ingrained scarcity beliefs. These beliefs can be so strong that they drive people to hoard massive amounts of money, chasing more without ever finding true fulfillment. True abundance is not about accumulation—it arises from embodying trust in our divine inner knowing. As we cultivate this trust, abundance flows through us naturally.

Sharing a conversation about abundance can be challenging as it has become so convoluted—many of us are still grappling with the true meaning, let alone how to live it. Ironically, the constant craving for abundance often undermines the very pathways to embodying it.

True abundance is not merely about having more than enough; it is rooted in reciprocity—the conscious exchange of giving and receiving.For those on the spiritual path of awakening, there can be a stigma around accumulating wealth, particularly in the form of money. This aversion often stems from the belief that financial gain is tied to exploitation or the fear of being judged for becoming wealthy. Both beliefs arise from a separation-based relationship with money.

In Unity, our connection to money shifts. As we grow and trust in abundance, we recognize that there is more than enough, and we see that manifesting money is directly linked to the flow within us.

Unity Belief
"Spirituality and abundance are synonymous with Unity."

Our outer reality mirrors our internal vibration and is shaped by the beliefs we hold to be true. If we believe money is tied to our purpose and also feel it is unattainable, we will manifest exactly that. When we allow our purpose—the flow of divinity—to guide us, we receive just what we need and often more, allowing us to feel secure in our abundance and able to share as our cup spills over.

While monetary wealth is certainly a form of abundance, it is important to remember that money is merely one form of it. Time spent being fully present—be it in nature, with family and friends, or pursuing a passion—is beyond what money could ever buy. Our time is precious. It is vital to recognize that abundance does not come from erroneous amounts of time chasing wealth, but rather from the quality of time. This shift allows our creative spark to thrive. Ideally, we can find a balance where our purpose is honored and abundance flows.

We currently live in a system where our work and our personal lives are separate. This division is repaired in the Unity paradigm as the two merge, forming in a Divine union—our purpose. As this new way takes root, we will see major changes reflecting this new reality. As the illusion of scarcity and separation dissolves, we will no longer need to pay others to raise our children or send them to be programmed by an outdated educational system initially built to enable parents to work during the rise of industrialization.

To be given the opportunity of manifesting true abundance, we must move away from the ceaseless programming of our culture. From there, we can believe that we are abundant just as we are, right where we are. This may feel daunting or even impossible if we are barely making ends meet—living paycheck to paycheck—caught believing there are not enough resources. Alternatively, we may have a great job that pays our expenses with money to spare, yet we feel a gaping hole as we long to follow our Divine purpose. Imagining abundance may feel difficult, but in time as our inner world and vibration shifts into Unity consciousness the possibilities will feel more tangible.

Some of us have to take the leap first, becoming examples for others to follow. Leaving behind a scarcity mindset can mean abandoning everything—no plan, no job, no home, and very little money—which can feel simultaneously liberating, terrifying, and exciting. It's like ripping off a band-aid: the faster we do it, the quicker the pain fades. In our most vulnerable times we are often given clear sight, revealing the chaos we had been living in, thus further inspiring us to break free. That said, we do not have to lose everything to do so. Timing is key.

Having a clear purpose is all that is required for accelerated growth in the Unity paradigm. However, if we are lacking direction—not yet clear on our life purpose—being in service can help resolve separation beliefs and in turn reveal our purpose.

When someone breaks away from the norm and acts in utter trust, those still trapped in fear may question their sanity or feel jealous, for the Divine within us wants nothing else than to live in faith. This reaction stems from separation programming and scarcity thinking. While it may be foreign, starting over is not as uncomfortable as living a lie or feeling stagnant in our evolution. Kudos to those who take these early leaps of faith! Staggering our leaps is necessary, for if everyone did it simultaneously there would be total chaos, which is not the intent. However, a certain degree of chaos will be unavoidable as we are entering an era of massive change. Abundance for all!

To envision abundance for all humans it starts within us. This is the only way real change can ever occur. To be truly abundant, we must have an unshakable belief that it is our birthright to have more than enough, to be fully provided for. This is not about accumulating an overabundance of material goods. Instead, it is about the freedom to express ourselves,

our purpose, and to live in service without concern for our
basic needs.

Abundance Practice

We cultivate an abundant vibration by envisioning our life in
abundance. Begin with gratitude and appreciation for what is
already present. These simple thoughts immediately elevate
the body's vibration, creating a foundation for expansion.

Take a moment to explore what a life of abundance feels like
for you. Where in your body do you sense abundance igniting?
Every feeling and emotion that arises is relevant—each one
deserves to be acknowledged and honored. Perhaps you notice
a sensation of openness or, conversely, a tightness somewhere
within. Simply observe.

Then, repeat the phrase: "I am abundant now."
When we fully embrace the belief of Unity—that we are always
abundant regardless of circumstances—we manifest
immediate abundance, even when we seemingly have nothing
to work with. How many times have we seen a mother or
caregiver whip together a delicious meal out of nothing? Using
what they have, they make miracles—grilled cheese with
blackberry jam!

This belief transforms our reality into one of abundance. Let
go of the idea that we have to wait to become abundant, for
this is yet another lie. We start at this very moment. In fact, it
is almost better to have nothing to lose, because when we have
something to lose we might convince ourselves that what we
have right now is the only thing that we are ever going to have.
Fueled by false fear, we stagnate in protection.

That said, growth does not have to be unduly painful. Many of
us have experienced lean times we do not wish to revisit. For

that reason, we seek security—expanding our reality while still honoring our sense of safety. Simply imagining a reality of abundance is already a profound and vital step.

As we resolve belief patterns rooted in separation and scarcity, we create fertile space within our energy body. Here, new Origin seeds are planted, forming an entire field of abundance. These seeds initiate new elemental patterns that naturally harmonize with life, resonating with our true nature—growing and expanding free from external corruption, such as the need for validation.

Nourished by the flow of Divine Love within us, our energetic vessel is reconstructed and strengthened. This process sustains higher vibrational frequencies, accelerating the manifestation of abundance in our lives. Over time, this internal transformation extends outward, ensuring abundance for all.

Unity Belief
"Scarcity is the lack of love &
abundance is Love's purest form."

Purpose

Abundance without purpose is not fulfilling and therefore is not true abundance. Allowing our authentic purpose to reveal itself to us is the next step to shift out of scarcity. It is the embodiment of separation beliefs that creates mindset, not the mind itself. As we begin to resolve separation belief patterns, the flow of Divinity increases in the body. From this new and higher vibration, we manifest a unique purpose that plays a specific role in the collective paradigm shift. As we step into our purpose we become a conduit. In turn, we manifest abundance for ourselves and everyone that experiences our Unity purpose.

The purpose we are given carries specific codes that will accelerate our awakening. It may come however as a great shift, encouraging us to embark on new horizons. Therefore, we may have to release what we had previously been doing in order to align with our new direction. Through this process, we learn to trust that there are new ways of being beyond what we have known and may recognize the honor that it is to have been given a Unity purpose to embody. Amid the blessings of this journey, we may face challenges as old belief patterns arise creating distractions and taunting us on our path.

From the neutrality of love, the Origin seed of our purpose takes root. From there, Divinely inspired ideas emerge. Remember, the whole universe is conspiring with us to ensure we manifest abundance for ourselves and beyond. The Divine purpose creates a golden template for us to follow.

The possibilities are endless. It could be altering our teaching style, writing a book, starting a podcast, developing a kid's camp, supporting sustainability efforts for Earth, feeding people in need healthy food, sharing alternative medicine practices, changing the structure of our workplace from within, or green building. The common thread between all these is that our purpose is designed to serve Unity and help others achieve abundance by also aligning with Unity.

Once we are certain of our purpose, everything changes. We begin to feel a focused calling that goes far beyond an idea as our souls are activated. We know we must follow this purpose to completion. The process of embodying our unique call becomes a fulfilling experience supported by synchronicities and emerging opportunities.

The essential leaps of faith make more "sense" and thus are easier to follow when we are connected to our unique purpose. Our purpose is created from Unity and since Unity is the essence of love and abundance, our purpose is inherently abundant. Being of service and supporting new Unity belief structures in our lives, be it in our jobs or relationships, can provide deep fulfillment and a powerful resiliency. While some people may need to make external changes such as the place they reside or the jobs and roles they hold, others may not need to make such changes and will experience their newfound purpose as an internal shift.

Commitment

Making a commitment to our purpose seals the deal and creates vibrational continuity that the universe understands. When we are indecisive and not fully committed, the universe reflects that uncertainty in our timelines. However, with consistent belief in our purpose and constant movement toward it, we begin to co-create synchronicities and opportunities. This is a key component in the flow of abundance. By making a commitment, we cultivate vibrational continuity that accelerates the manifestation of our purpose. This energy ripples outward, informing the Universal Mind thus creating a crystalline structure. From that structure an elemental pattern. The commitment to the purpose accelerates the emerging blueprint of the golden template. This process generates magnetism in the body, creating timelines filled with opportunities that make it easier to manifest abundance. Since the essence of manifestation is vibrational, the more conviction and repetition we infuse into our thoughts, words, and actions related to our purpose, the faster manifestation occurs.

It is through our commitment to purpose that we strengthen the vibrational container of the energetic body. We begin to gather confidence and resilience with a strong unshakable commitment. This vibration attracts what we need to manifest our purpose. We can no longer rely on the way things have been to make decisions since following old patterns inhibits our evolution. This requires great courage and a dedication to radical honesty to bear witness to the illusions that attempt to deter us.

Action

We cannot passively watch life unfold from the comfort of our couch—we must take action! Life is movement, a continuous unfolding of experiences, and we are meant to engage with it fully. And for the sake of joy, may we embrace the process with curiosity and playfulness. The Universe is in constant interaction and co-creation within us, responding to every thought, every step, and every intention we put forth.

To honor this co-creative dance, we must step into our role as active participants. If we feel uncertain about the "right" direction or caught in the hesitation of beginning, let us remember: any action is better than none. Movement dissolves stagnation, and even the smallest step can shift our trajectory. The Universe does not require perfection—only our willingness to engage. Every step taken in alignment with our purpose is met with reciprocity, for action is the physical embodiment of our relationship with nature.

This is where the rubber meets the road—where thought becomes form, where energy turns into experience. The signs are always present, guiding us toward abundance, but we must be willing to listen. Listen to the inner knowing, the subtle cues pulling us forward. Pay attention to the quiet nudges, the synchronicities, the moments of inspiration that whisper, this way. These signals are the language of abundance, ever-present, ever-calling us into deeper alignment with the life we are meant to live.

Another Abundance Practice

Every Morning: Begin your day by creating a gratitude list. Reflect on the blessings, both big and small, that already exist in your life. Gratitude shifts your focus from scarcity to abundance.

Giving & Receiving: Practice both giving and receiving with yourself. Notice which one feels easier—do you find it more natural to give, or to receive? Feel any resistance that arises. Follow that resistance back to its origin, the seed of that belief pattern, and allow it to be seen. Simply witnessing it can create space for transformation.

Acts of Kindness: Help strangers, friends, or family with a kind word or gesture, expecting nothing in return. This could be as simple as offering encouragement, holding space for someone, or sharing something meaningful. Do this in a way that does not deplete your own energy, but rather sustains and uplifts you as well.

Aligned Action: Each day, take one small step toward your purpose. It does not have to be grand—what matters is consistency. Even the smallest action can shift momentum, opening the path for abundance to flow naturally.

Herbal Insights: Dandelion & Mint

☽ **Best Ways to Connect:** Tea | Tincture | Nature Connection

🌿 **Dandelion** *(Taraxacum officinale)* — A potent ally for releasing scarcity mindsets, dandelion embodies resilience, exuberance, and perseverance. This vibrant plant never gives up! Sitting beside them in a yard, meadow, or anywhere she grows offers an opportunity to listen. Speak to her, ask for support in strengthening your purpose, and find the courage to take action even in the face of resistance. Dandelion detoxifies stagnant energy by moving it out of the body.

🌱 **Mint** *(Mentha spp.)* — A known attractor of abundance, mint uplifts the mind and encourages fresh perspectives. They thrive in nearly any condition, reminding us that opportunities and prosperity are always within reach. With her bright, invigorating energy, mint and her plant allies offer clarity, confidence, and ease as you move forward.

CHAPTER SEVEN

THE LIVING EARTH

*EARTH IS A LIVING, BREATHING ENTITY—AN
ORGANISM TEEMING WITH AN ABUNDANCE
OF INTERCONNECTED DIVERSE LIFE.*

Mother Earth is a living, breathing miracle. Her biodiverse ecosystems are brilliant and beautiful. Harmoniously weaving together plants, animals and the elements, She is Unity. This intricate tapestry rhythmically ebbs and flows, creating the interconnected web of life.

Each living being, from the tiniest microbe to the vast whales and redwoods, is significant and has a unique purpose. Since every organism is interdependent, our survival depends on one another.

We are nature.

Within the folds of Gaia's energetic body lies holographic imprints, holding many secrets and ancient knowledge that await our exploration. The depth of these parallel realities is infinite. We may find plant spirits, animal spirits, ancestors, and countless beings of light that reside within these folds. This can be referred to as the subtle realms.

The sacredness of nature crackles with purity and benevolence. When we remember to enter into a sacred communion with nature we align with our true nature.

Every human carries unique ancestral ties to ancient indigenous people. While these connections may feel distant, the thread can never be cut. We can find inspiration and wisdom in the practices of indigenous peoples, for many have maintained a reciprocal relationship with nature amid our changing modern world. Many indigenous cultures have been holding the Origin seed of Unity safe for thousands of years. They are the keepers of the light.

Our current society has much to remember regarding our relationship with life beyond ourselves and those we hold in our immediate circle. How we have treated nature in recent times serves as a potent reflection of how we treat ourselves, demonstrating the grave disconnect we have adopted.

As we merge with our inner knowing, we are irresistibly drawn back to the wilds of nature.

It is understandable to feel anger, sadness and grief as the illusion of separation begins to lift. The deep programming that led to the belief that we are not nature and the attempt to disempower the feminine has created deep wounds in all humans. It is equivalent to ripping a newborn away from her mother.

Nature is the best medicine to heal wounds of separation. Go seek refuge with our original and eternal mother. Don't wait—be it a walk to the back yard or simply opening a highrise window and letting the breeze in—do it now!

As we attune to the rhythmic flow of the elements, something magical happens within us. Our senses unite, leading us to a space of serene balance. Whether it is the winding journey alongside a babbling brook or the awe of a magnificent tree—the spirits purify the illusion of separation and we begin to surrender to the unfolding.

We listen intently to the Water, the ethereal songs of birds, and the whispering Wind. With the Earth beneath us and the sun's warmth above, we open and embrace healing, anchored in our larger existence. Amid life's relentless flow, nature's embrace offers solace—a haven of safety and calm.

In nature's embrace, we fully experience and honor all emotions by yielding to tranquility and the slow passage of time. Inside us resides the wisdom of the serpent, the eagle's soaring spirit, and the condor's grace. We sway like blossoms in the breeze, aligned with the owl's ancient wisdom and the hawk's powerful call.

By listening to our inner waters—our inner knowing—we awaken our wild, raw expression of passion, echoing the wolf's moonlit howl and embodying the mountain lion's decisive leadership.

Together, we will heal the wounds of separation.

The mountains are alive—each one carrying their own distinct energy field, unique and specific to their story and place. Their wisdom is ancient and sacred. When we open ourselves to them, we can commune in a reverent and reciprocal way—not seeking to gain, we see how we can give. When we retreat to the mountains, it is as though we are cradled by the nurturing embrace of the Great Mother—allowing our weary bodies to rest and recover in her arms. The mountains stand timeless, steadfast in their presence they support all of nature. As containers for life they shape the land and guide Water down from their peaks, giving sustenance to everything below.

From the solidity of the mountains to the vast openness of the desert, we find unique demonstrations of beauty—all steeped in the neutrality of love. In the desert's expansive silence, we sit amidst the howling winds of the day and the infinite quiet of the night. The desert offers us space, reminding us of our own inner wisdom that often goes unnoticed in the busyness of daily life. It is in the stillness and solitude of this vastness that we come face to face with ourselves and witness the rise of the serpent energy within, symbolizing the awakening of deeper truths.

As we journey from the desert to the rhythmic shores of the ocean, we invite yet another form of nature's cleansing. The beaches, with their endless waves crashing against ancient cliffs, call us to spend a few days in their embrace. The sound of the ocean tides, in their constant ebb and flow, gently washes over us, helping to dissolve any lingering obscurations. In this space, the rhythm of the sea becomes a powerful ally, guiding us to release what no longer serves, leaving us refreshed and renewed.

Earth grounding meditation

Come to a tranquil space outside to commune with the living Earth. Before settling, maybe ask if your presence is welcome. Then take a moment to arrive. Remove your shoes, feel the Earth beneath your feet. Stand or sit comfortably grounding—Earthing—your body. Relax the jaw, face and shoulders. Allow yourself to feel held.

Visualize roots extending from the soles of your feet and body. Feel these roots anchoring you to the ground. Sense the vibrant energy of Gaia flowing up through your roots and into your body. Allow her to create a rhythm within you.

As you connect with the Earth's rhythms, allow yourself to feel a sense of oneness and Unity with the planet. Listen to the sounds of nature—a song composed by this moment that will never play again.

When you are ready, slowly open your eyes. Look around to see the small wonders happening everywhere: insects buzzing, birds flying, trees swaying, dogs playing, children crying, Water flowing, Wind blowing. Attune to whatever lies within the scope of your senses.

Now, enter a *deep appreciation* for each of those little miracles. What would life be like if they weren't there? Remember, you too are one of those miracles!

Green Nation

We would not be alive without our rooted kin.

These abundant beings already live in Unity. Sometimes it can even feel as though they are here to care for us—to teach us. Each plant species possesses a unique intelligence, purpose, and personality. The assumption that they lack consciousness hinders us from building relationships with them, reinforcing the false idea that we are separate from or better than them.

While they do not have a brain like most animals, they communicate, feel vibrations, and respond to praise. Plants skillfully present their spirit and personality to humans so we can connect with them.

Can we learn to communicate and have harmonious relationships with them?

The answer is that we already communicate and have relationships with them. However, since the illusion of separation is strong we often feel we cannot enter the exchange or go so far to believe plants are here for us to use and abuse them.

The first fundamental law of nature is that we all need each other. It is through our collective cooperation and reverence for each other that we begin to awaken Unity within us.

The healing effects we receive from plants and herbs are not mere coincidences. These plants *want* to help us heal. They remember and embody the fundamental law of interdependence. They love us. And when we offer them love in return, they respond in kind.

Our bodies have specific receptors designed to interact seamlessly with plant compounds. For example, we have cannabinoid receptors that naturally engage with cannabinoids in the cannabis plant. These receptors are part of the endocannabinoid system and play an important role in regulating our mood, pain, and other physiological processes. Another notable example is the vanilloid receptor type 1 (TRPV1), also known as the capsaicin receptor, found in Cayenne pepper. TRPV1 receptors regulate metabolism and body temperature, our perception of pain, serve as antihistamines, and can prevent cancer.

By looking to the higher intelligence that created these brilliant, symbiotic systems between humans and plants, we are reminded that we are One Love.

The Green Nation is guided by a higher purpose and originates from and is the essence of Unity. Plants showcase remarkable adaptability to unique and varied environments that they inhabit. With an innate sense of abundance and an altruistic dedication to service, they embody the complex web of life. In turn, they have the ability to channel immense flows of information that then direct and animate them.

Plant wisdom goes far beyond the narrow confines of Allopathic pharmaceutical research. The pervasive reductionist approach, which isolates specific components from each plant and then synthetically replicates them, fails to honor the profound interconnectedness and complex intelligence of the plant itself.

This ideation, stemming from the separation paradigm, reflects the complex relationship between scientific research for-profit corporations. Current research is largely influenced by where there is money and since minimal profit would come from recognizing the wisdom of whole plant allies, versus their isolated parts, resources are rarely allocated to studying this. While

Western medicine and pharmaceuticals certainly have a time and place and can save lives, we lose significant gifts if we solely focus our energy there. There is no reason to not integrate both approaches into a holistic healthcare system.

Plant Allies

Every human has specific plant allies, whether we are aware of them or not. These allies are conscious of us, they are alive. Each plant species has a unique spirit possessing great intelligence. Plant spirits are trusted companions. Having been in relationship with us for lifetimes, they help resolve patterns we carry from previous lives.

For instance, a dandelion has an energetic spirit. Think of cartwheels and a sunny disposition filled with resilience and tenacity. Dandelion supports liver detoxification and infuses the system with vitality. If our liver needs tending, dandelions will often grow around us in abundance communicating they are here for us. Likewise, plants that mitigate toxins often grow in wastelands that need restoration—ready to aid and repair the ecosystem.

Consider Mugwort, a protector and a connector to the subtle realms. Shamans, priestesses, and healers of all kinds have built relationships with Mugwort for eons. She often grows around homes and when encountering her, we might experience a deep sense of recognition, as though we are reuniting with family.

Burdock tends to grow in soil that needs cleansing. Thus Burdock might be a choice ally for those in need of grounding energy. If we carry attachments that need to be released, Burdock burrs may cling to our clothing while hiking, gently nudging us to clear our energetic field. On a physical level, Burdock is high in inulin (a prebiotic that supports the gut microbiome), is known to cleanse the liver, aid in digestion, and detoxify the blood.

Given we have a profound resonance with these allies, whether conscious of the connection or not, we can be greatly impacted by them. For instance, the sight or scent of Lilac or Peppermint might evoke an inexplicable sense of joy. Alternatively, coming into contact with a Birch tree could awaken dormant memories. Such experiences underscore the deep, mystical bond between humans and the natural world.

Our botanical allies are constantly extending invitations to us to further enhance our connection with them. The process of transforming our interactions with plants and trees into cherished friendships is an ancient practice that is frequently overlooked (or even doubted) in our current culture. That said, there are people today who comprehend this connection and live in deep communion with the plant spirits.

As we become more attuned to our plant allies and nurture our relationships with them, our connection with nature deepens.
The plants themselves are keen to learn from us and actively participate in our collective awakening. The plant kingdom—or kindom—possesses its own consciousness that is evolving alongside humanity. Every being on Earth, not just humans, is destined to experience a frequency shift as we move into Unity.

Psychedelics

The world is turning its attention to psychedelic plant medicines for compelling reasons. These ancient gifts from nature serve as powerful catalysts for transformation, accelerating personal growth by offering glimpses into the vast, interconnected realms of consciousness. Plants like Ayahuasca, Iboga, Mescaline, and Psilocybin hold the ability to lift the veil of separation, allowing us to perceive reality in a profoundly different way. They invite us to unravel stagnant patterns, dissolve illusions, and step into deeper alignment with our true nature.

These sacred plants are now reaching nearly every corner of the world through ceremonial settings, where their spirits act as wise guides. They dwell close to the Divine in ways beyond human comprehension, carrying the ability to facilitate deep healing and aid in the awakening process. Those who feel called to these medicines are often given the opportunity to clear lifetimes of stagnation and break free from limiting cycles. However, the integration process that follows is just as important as the experience itself—yet it is often overlooked. Taking time to sit with what arises, whether in solitude, journaling, or speaking with trusted allies, is essential. The work truly begins after the ceremony, in how we embody the insights received.

Despite the undeniable therapeutic potential of these plants, cultural and political resistance remains strong. Modern scientific research continues to explore and validate their benefits, dismantling the long-held myth that they are inherently dangerous. Studies show that, when used in supportive and intentional settings, these medicines can be profoundly effective in repatterning emotional trauma and expanding personal awareness. Yet, misinformation persists—largely fueled by efforts to protect pharmaceutical profits, reinforcing a false narrative of fear. Ironically, when approached with care and respect, these plant medicines have fewer risks and complications than many allopathic treatments.

The key to receiving the true benefits of psychedelic plant medicines lies in reverence, intention, and responsible guidance. These are not substances for escape, but rather tools for deep exploration. If you feel called, seek the wisdom of a trained practitioner—one who has cultivated a true relationship with the plant spirit and understands the depth of the work ahead. With the right preparation, support, and integration, these ancient allies can illuminate the path toward healing, connection, and awakening.

Mushrooms

A big bow, to our fungal allies the mushrooms! These celestial gifts descended from the cosmos, took root in Earth's soil, and emerged into sight. Mycelium networks are one of the most profound living technologies, creating the foundation for our ecosystems and all of life.

Mushrooms are versatile healers. Species like Lion's Mane, Reishi, and Cordyceps offer therapeutic benefits that enhance human well-being and vitality. They also serve as environmental caretakers, breaking down toxic waste aiding Earth's rejuvenation.

As science continues to "prove" their potential, mushroom's multi-faceted healing properties will be recognized and thus integrated into mainstream medicine.

Connect to Plants Spirit-Practice

In a moment, go outside and allow yourself to feel drawn to a tree or plant. Take a moment to greet it, either with spoken words or through silent thoughts. Gently make contact by touching the plant—share your energy and breathe with it. Express your intention to cultivate a relationship and your desire to listen and learn from this living being.

Engage in a quiet conversation of stillness. Let your senses attune to any messages that arise. Remain open—ready to receive thoughts, visions, or feelings that emerge as you commune with the plant spirit.

When you feel ready, express gratitude to your plant friend for its presence and wisdom. Acknowledge your budding relationship and the potential for ongoing communication and growth.

Take a moment to absorb and integrate the experience and return to yourself. If your eyes were closed, gently open them returning to the immediate environment. Awaken your sense of hearing, attune to the soundscape—acknowledging the other life forms and elements that surround you.

Wonderfully, we do not need to be in wild places to connect with plant allies. Whether inside the house, walking down a city street, or drinking herbal tea, there are endless opportunities to expand our relationship with our plant-kin.

Herbal Insights: Nettle & Red Clover

☽ **Best Ways to Connect: Tea | Tincture | Nature Connection**

🌿 **Nettle** *(Urtica dioica)* Nettle is a true representation of the vitality of the Earth. It's a robust and resilient plant, full of life force, known for its ability to nourish, detoxify, and invigorate the body. Nettle thrives in fertile soil and connects deeply with the Earth's rhythms, making it an excellent ally for grounding and cleansing the energetic and physical body.

🌺 **Red Clover** *(Trifolium pratense)* Red clover is deeply connected to the Earth and known for its ability to purify the blood, enhance fertility, and strengthen the body's natural healing abilities. Its rich, vibrant blossoms serve as a reminder of the regenerative power of nature, encouraging us to open up to the flow of abundance and health.

CHAPTER EIGHT

UNITY LANGUAGE

*HOW WE SPEAK IS A CO-CREATIVE PRAYER.
EVERY WORD HAS A UNIQUE VIBRATIONAL SIGNATURE·
WHAT DO WE WISH TO SPEAK INTO EXISTENCE?*

The human voice carries incredible power. Each time we speak, we are co-creating our reality with the Divine as every word is recorded in the Universal Mind and thus every word is a prayer. As we speak, the infinite pool of Love listens in neutrality. For instance, we always receive what we ask for; however, it rarely manifests how the mind imagined. This is the Great Mystery.

Each word has a Origin seed, purpose, and specific vibrational signature that has evolved over time. When a word is spoken the vibration carries the unique intention that dwells within the harmonics of the word. The vibrational continuity and power of the word is entirely dependent on the person speaking the word, namely what they intend to communicate beyond the word itself—their energetic intention.

The way we speak, our tone, and the intention behind our words shapes the reality we experience. Our words are powerful. When we speak with clarity, our words gain the potential to either attract abundance or manifest scarcity in our lives. The energy and conviction behind a word amplify its potency, creating a continuity in our bodies that resonates with the frequency of our intentions. This vibrational continuity is like a rhythm or resonance that aligns with our purpose, reinforcing our commitment to embodying it. Our words, whether directed to one person or an entire audience, are woven into the fabric of universal consciousness—the Universal Mind. This collective energy field can amplify our words when they resonate with those who hear them. For instance, when we speak to a group of people who feel our authenticity and align with our message, the vibrational impact of our words is magnified. Words spoken from a place of neutrality and love resonate deeply, creating powerful and positive shifts. Alternatively, words born from fear or hatred--despite originating from Love-may manifest negative outcomes since they stem from a contracted fearful state. born from fear or hatred manifesting negative separation outcomes.

The Universal Mind is an impartial mirror, simply reflecting back the energy we emit. Embodying the neutrality of love, the Universal Mind responds to both energies--positive and negative--without judgment; however, words rooted in love tend to bring forth a greater sense of harmony, wholeness, and alignment into our lives. Recognizing that love is the true origin of all words, even those that communicate separation, can be a transformative perspective for it begins to erode and diminish the power of negative words. However, this can be challenging to remember, given that language has become convoluted by associations, personal experiences, and societal influences. Even a word that seems universally positive such as "love," can carry mixed or even painful meanings due to the personal and collective filters it passes through.

Our words are tragically diluted in the separation paradigm. This outdated reality encourages "sameness" at the expense of authenticity and raw expression. This stagnation contributes to increasing entropy and dissatisfaction in our lives. It may feel as though we are in a trance, afraid to say anything outside the norm. Given many people still live under the veil of separation, when we speak of love or share insights from our inner knowing they can be rejected. Unfortunately, denying or dismissing Unity beliefs further entrenches the illusion and can hinder an individual from feeling safe to share emerging Unity perspectives in the future.

Our current culture is deeply enmeshed with Separation beliefs and tragically we are actively perpetuating this paradigm. Since this is the water we are swimming in, most ideas, language, and actions are tethered to Separation. How have we become so constrained and tainted as a species? This suppression is undoubtedly harming us, hindering our evolution, and killing our spirits. Fortunately, Unity is emerging within us.

The manner and content of our speech directly affects how we interface with all facets of life—seen and unseen. Interwoven into the harmonics of our voice is the love and light of our soul, family, and lineage, as well as myriad life experiences from dis-ease and illness, to past trauma, to our current emotional state. When we experience gratitude or joy, the vibration resonates through our words. Conversely, when we feel fear or insecurity correlating energy is expressed through our tone and word choice.

Whoever we are speaking with can sense this in various ways. We have the ability to "hear" beyond our ears, for we process information with our heart and gut. Our biofield acts as a receptor, capturing valuable information, transcending the separation paradigm. We intuitively assess whether someone is trustworthy, authentic, or safe. These gauges are more superficial and survival based, and barely scratch the surface of the complex exchange of information between two people in conversation. As we move beyond the illusion of separation, we recognize the value in every interaction. Every individual has a piece of the puzzle to offer through their words. We begin to perceive that beyond the thorns, lives a rose; beyond the fear, there is love. By truly listening to the meaning of words, beyond their definition, and by allowing our lens of separation to weaken, we can see the beautiful light that shines through all Beings.

The human voice possesses a profound and enigmatic power that reaches far beyond mere communication. It is the instrument through which we express our emotions, convey our thoughts, and forge connections with others. And it is in this realm of connection that the voice reveals its most

extraordinary ability—the capacity to resonate with others on an intuitive level.

When we meet someone new, we often form an immediate

impression based on their voice. Within moments, we can sense whether we feel drawn to them or not. This instant recognition is not simply a matter of personal preference or even the words they use. It is an energetic response that is deeply rooted in our body.

The human voice is produced by the vocal cords, two bands of tissue that stretch across the larynx when we speak. The shape and size of these cords determine the pitch and tone of our voice. Interestingly, the vocal cords bear a striking resemblance to the vagina in their physical appearance, both consisting of soft, elastic tissue that expands and contracts. This similarity is not coincidental. Rather, it is a reflection of the profound connection between the voice and the womb.

Just as the womb is the Origin seed of human life, the voice is the birthplace of sound, and sound is the birthplace of the universe we live in. When we speak, we are not simply producing vibrations of air. We are giving birth to acoustic creations that shape our reality. These sounds can uplift, inspire, comfort, and heal. They can also divide, deceive, and destroy. The choice of how we engage with our voice is an immense responsibility to never take lightly. That said, when Separation is deeply ingrained it can be challenging to "choose" what we express. In time, awareness can grow from vibrational upgrades and from here we may feel more resourced to enact change to further embody Unity.

It's curious how we often find it easier to discuss problems in a lazy, habitual way that makes them seem unchangeable, rather than engage in conversations focused on potential solutions that require action. When we express beliefs rooted in separation, we reinforce their vibrational continuity, cementing them in our collective consciousness and solidifying the very opposite of what we wish to achieve. Every word we speak ripples out indefinitely. By voicing separation beliefs into the field, we invite others to join in our naïve, misguided, and stagnant mindset. The saying "misery loves company" exists for a reason—energy is contagious.

We are not here to police words! The intent is to increase awareness about the power and energy of speech. No one likes being told how to speak, it only creates further division. The invitation is to pause and come into neutrality for a moment before speaking. Feel the intonation, quality, and flow of the words as they arise. Learning to craft Unity language takes practice, for it is not just the words that matter, but also the intention behind the words we choose.

Like anything, this practice requires patience. It can be challenging to speak in alignment with our true nature for it may feel uncomfortably foreign and thus unknown and even scary. Once we have gained clarity about the importance of authentic speech, offering others grace and compassion as they embark on learning how to speak in Unity. If we meet them with impatience, judgment, or condescending remarks we will greatly inhibit their growth. Alternatively, by offering an intentional and loving response we can uplift the individual encouraging them on their path of purpose. We can offer the same grace to ourselves.

The way we speak is shaped by our sense of flow and the influence of our education. When people describe someone as well-spoken, they usually mean that the person communicates clearly, fluently, and articulately.

Cultivating discernment between authentic and articulate speech arises from a well-balanced inner knowing. While both can coexist, for the sake of our evolution, we can practice speaking authentically and in alignment with our Unity purpose. Speaking "well" (i.e., clearly, fluently, and articulately) does not necessarily mean we are contributing something new or unique to the conversation, or even to ourselves. For instance, we may rely on quoting others to mask our fear of speaking from the heart, which disrupts the natural flow of our Divinity. As we learn to trust our inner knowing and speak from the neutrality of love, words begin to flow naturally—not from the mind but from the heart—from this place we enter a flow state, where words arise to be both understood and felt in their most complete and natural form. There is no need to filter or curate our speech for external validation, as we trust in our innate worthiness and communicate in ways that resonate within a Unity vibration..

The intellectual or spiritual ego can easily fall into habits of repeating knowledge that we have not yet fully embodied.... While this may not seem harmful, it limits our ability to speak from a place of true personal power. In these moments, we might unknowingly engage in spiritual bypassing, avoiding the deeper work of integrating knowledge into lived experience. True growth comes from moving beyond simply repeating words that we have read or learned from another and stepping into the embodiment of that wisdom. When we speak from a place of authentic embodiment, our words carry deeper vibrational integrity, aligning with the harmonics of truth. This authenticity allows for communication that conveys greater power, depth, and Unity within the words we speak.

Without judgment, invite inquiry into our daily conversations and notice what patterns emerge. How much of our conversations fixate on what's wrong with the world? Do we often shift blame to others or institutions, like the government, for the reality we face? Do we speak reactively, out of habit, instead of fully listening to the person we are engaging with? How often do we repeat words and phrases mindlessly, without pausing to reflect on their meaning and impact (i.e., "It is what it is" or "I'd rather poke my eyes out")? How often do we take the time to encourage others, taking the spotlight off ourselves? We might begin to identify which of our words are rooted in separation and create a divide compared to those that promote Unity, both within ourselves and with the people we connect with.

Our words and thoughts have a powerful impact on the reality we create. When we constantly talk about what we do not want, we are unintentionally manifesting those unwanted things into our lives. This happens because repetition creates a vibrational pattern that is acted on within the Universal Mind, forming timelines that align with the vibrational continuity we are creating. If we are not aware of our words and thoughts, we may manifest limitations, perpetuating a cycle of scarcity.

For instance, when we say things like, "It probably won't work out" or "I will never make money from my art" or "I have the worst luck," we are unknowingly programming our internal system to align with exactly what we fear. The impact of these words is influenced by the degree of energy we place behind them and how often we repeat them. If we occasionally release these self-defeating thoughts out of frustration, they do not hold the same vibrational power, especially if we do not believe they are fundamentally true. Remember, it is the continual repetition of self-defeating phrases that manifests scarcity, embedding said beliefs deeply into our body. There is no need for shame in these moments, for sometimes we experience and express temporary frustration. Ideally though, we can observe the occurrence, continuing to build our muscle of awareness.

With purpose, we find a passion that increases the flow state in the body. With commitment, we cultivate repetition when we speak of our purpose, thus creating fertile ground for change. In turn, this establishes the vibrational continuity in our words and phrases, creating a clear invitation to the field of potentiality, thus indicating our readiness and openness to receive abundant flows of connection. While affirmations certainly assist this process, the most effective way to break patterns of separation is to weave Unity into every word we utter.

Finding purpose and resolving separation beliefs naturally increases the brain's neuroplasticity, which in turn releases habitual phrases and words that we have been looping. As we further embrace Unity consciousness, we incorporate words and phrases that align with our unique purpose and reveal our truth to the world.

Free speech is a universal human right that should be upheld for everyone. Historically, language filters were developed during times when it was unsafe to express oneself fully. Unfortunately, this remains true in many parts of the world today. When we speak from the Unity within us, genuine free speech can occur even in oppressive situations. We advocate for free speech by speaking from the neutrality of love, there is nothing more powerful for we are manifestors and creators of Unity.

When we communicate in Unity compared to polarizing, fear based dogmas, we can create solutions for myriad imbalances. It is important as we change our language to not become rigid, for that is the antithesis of Unity. Unity language is vast and thus is accepting of slang and cultural linguistics that allow us to express our individuality. If we feel called to use colorful language or even swear we can, so long as the intention behind whatever we are communicating is rooted in Unity.

In a world drowning in extreme polarity, it is the love and equanimity behind our words that can foster meaningful communication and thus change. By possessing the ability to convey our message without invalidating those who hold opposing beliefs, we enter the complex expanse of Unity. Surpassing the notion that "sameness" grants acceptance, we can find common ground amid great differences—the very medicine our divisive times necessitates. Furthermore, deep listening rooted in neutrality, allows us to tap into our Divinity while speaking and helps us honor the Divine of whoever we are conversing with.

Speaking with people that we disagree with can be a powerful way to enhance and expand our compassionate speech.

We learn to not be rigid and overly attached to our perspective—leaving room for varying opinions— while not diminishing ourselves or our truths.

The truth is, blame and shame are perpetuated from within us. The challenge is to acknowledge that these lower vibrational states, which emerge covertly or consciously in our thoughts and words, can be very hurtful to others. To change this, we need to confront how we internalize our own blame and shame. The self-defeating thoughts that manifest as words can begin to resolve naturally as we embody Unity.

Whenever we speak as if we are superior to others, we reinforce the paradigm of separation and inflate our spiritual egos. Embracing the truth of innate equality, we liberate our speech and resolve countless separation belief patterns.

Unity speech is Unifying.

Certain words can create ambiguity and a lack of vibrational continuity. What are we really communicating by saying, "Um... I think so," or "maybe," or "sort of"? Although these words have their time and place, they can be overused and therefore require greater attention. Phrases such as these tend to communicate self-doubt, insecurity, and fear of perception versus a grounded self-confidence.

When we take the time to expand our opinions and speech to include words that articulate Unity, we are planting seeds in whoever we are speaking with. While it is ultimately up to them whether or not the seeds take root, there is a higher chance they will respond in kind and match our Unity vibration. After sharing an expansive and unifying conversation, ideally both parties feel heard and inspired.

Language is a powerful thing. While it can be a beautiful vessel for love and genuine connection, it can also carry the weight of our insecurities and desires for validation—habits picked up along the way to protect ourselves. Because of this, our words can imbue subtle tones of manipulation, without conscious intention or even awareness that we are trying to steer a situation in our favor. We've all been there, caught in patterns of speech that do not align with our true nature and are influenced by fears and beliefs rooted in scarcity. By journeying toward radical honesty and authenticity, we are able to move beyond these patterns and express ourselves more clearly and lovingly.

We may encounter people who speak the language of Unity but have not yet fully embodied its integrity. It is important to meet these moments with both compassion and discernment. Some may use Unity-based speech as a form of manipulation, especially those still living deep in their woundedness. Recognizing this, we must remember that words can serve as both a bridge to connection and a shield of protection.

As we listen, we can tune into the truth behind the words by noticing how they resonate within us. This invites us to examine the feelings that arise—whether insecurity, scarcity, or something else—offering us the opportunity to process them through the lens of Unity rather than separation. Our responses to words originate from within us, making it essential to cultivate awareness of our own internal landscape.

By deepening our awareness of language, we learn to speak from the heart, allowing love and sincerity to be our guide. In doing so, we honor the true purpose of words—to connect, uplift, and support one another, free from ego or agenda.

Toxic positivity speech refers to individuals insistent on solely acknowledging the bright side at the expense of recognizing the unavoidable flip side—the shadow. When overly attached to this mode of being, people often correct or dismiss other perspectives that express darker truths. This mindset unjustly ignores the reality that life can be challenging and unfair. We live in a world that can be cruel and dark as well as beautiful; therefore, relentless positivity is not always appropriate. Sometimes, expressing our feelings about the challenging aspects of life is refreshing, necessary, and validating of our experiences.

In moments of authentic vulnerability, we discover the language of love. Sharing our true feelings, especially those of struggles and pain, can give others the permission and encouragement to do the same—truth is contagious! Speaking honestly about how we feel and listening as others express themselves, even if their sharing stems from separation, aids our collective shift into Unity. Within the container of speaking our truth, it is important to avoid excessive blaming of others or ourselves, as the ultimate healing comes from within. However, in the case of violence or abuse, we may need to identify the role of a perpetrator in causing harm. The question then becomes, can we do so without layering blame and shame onto the individual and instead see their harmful and inexcusable actions as an outcome of their own undigested pain? The process of forgiveness and healing can be incredibly complex. All in all, balancing honesty, raw vulnerability, and responsibility within our speech opens the door to authentic relating with others as well as with disowned parts of ourselves.

As we begin trusting our ability to speak from our inner knowing, we open ourselves to integrating words and insights from the neutrality of love. Our inner Divinity often becomes available to us in ways we could not have previously imagined. It can be surprising to find ourselves using unfamiliar words or discovering knowledge we did not know we have access to. Further, sharing our Divine insights in everyday conversations can catch others off guard, this may induce a reaction from their uncomfortableness. From that place they may try to diminish or infuse what-about-isms into the conversations so they may stay in the familiar-known, and therefore may make us resistant to sharing our divinity, Developing deep self-trust, recognizing the power within us, and trusting it is safe to express our truths encourages us to align with the changes that have been initiated within us. When conversations evolve into exchanges of Divinity, we move beyond merely reciting external knowledge. We stand on the brink of a linguistic evolution and revolution.

Deep Dive

Sounds created by our voices possess the remarkable ability to support healing within our bodies. By tuning to the energetic imbalances that create blockages within us, we can learn to mimic the sound of the specific blockages and direct the vibrations to the area of dis-ease or tension with great intention and attention. This simple act of sounding can begin to dissolve blockages and restore the body's natural energy flow. Just as an opera singer shatters a wine glass by matching its resonant frequency, we can resonate with points of trauma, pain, or dis-ease within—"shattering" stagnant energy to restore balance.

Sound healing aligns with resonance theory, which suggests that all matter, including our bodies, vibrates at specific frequencies. When these frequencies become disrupted—due to trauma, stress, or illness—energetic blockages are likely to form.

By creating vocal sounds that match the frequencies of these blockages, we create vibrational patterns that help free stagnation, effectively "re-tuning" the affected areas to our current desired frequency.

Consistency is key for this process to be effective. Repeating sound practices over time allows us to clear deeply ingrained blockages. As we continue, our energy begins to flow more freely and the potency of our vocal tones becomes more focused and precise, akin to a laser. Studies on sound healing techniques such as toning, chanting, and humming show that vocalization can increase vagal tone, reduce stress markers, and improve immune function. These physiological shifts demonstrate the profound effects of sound not only as an emotional release, but also as a tool for physical healing. This emergent research reminds us of the interconnection between emotional and physical health and the underlying presence of vibration within all aspects of life.

This approach to vocal sound healing, with repetition and mindful intention, enables us to break up stagnant energy and re-establish the body's natural rhythms. We can practice this right now! Next time we have a pain or are diagnosed with a dis-ease we can use our voices to help remedy the ailment. Wonderfully there is no downside to practicing this incredible and "free" technique that lives within us.

Take the time to listen to the blockage—sense into the quality, the sounds of the stuck energy. Connect to the Origin seed of the elemental pattern of the blockage. From this place of presence, allow the resonant sound to emerge. The sound may feel dissonant if it is the true re-creation and expression of a dis-ease. Slowly mimic the sound—allowing the vibration to

114

suffuse and shake up the blockage. After a few moments, shift to a harmonious sound and call upon any allies to express through your voice—the voice of Unity. This will bring healing light into the area of the body that is asking for support—to be resolved. The most important part of this practice, as with any practice, lives in the repetition.

In finding and embodying the Unity voice, we learn to trust our untapped healing potential. The potential of the human voice is boundless. The future of voice as a creative force isn't far-off—it's already here, ready to shape reality in ways we're only beginning to explore. We can co-create elemental patterns that shape our experiences and manifest our world. Through the use of sound we can generate toroidal fields—the omnipresent dynamic and self-sustaining energy structures that surround and support all life forms. We can invite the spirits of plants, ancestors, ascended masters, and even our higher selves to flow through the sounds we create to further amplify our healing intentions. As a result, this can infuse profound levels of consciousness into our creations.

By including these spiritual forces in our affirmations and aligning our voices with the energies of the earth and cosmos, we enter potent and vast realms of manifestation. As we deepen our trust in the immense powers within us, we might even influence fundamental forces that govern physical reality, like gravity itself!

This vision far surpasses the boundaries of known science. Much about the power of voice and the potential for a Unity language remains uncharted. Such ideas of a foreign new reality are Origin seeds barely beginning to sprout. They offer glimpses into the extraordinary paradigm shift we are co-creating. All possibilities, dreams, and "far fetched" realities begin with our willingness to believe, explore, and create from the depths of our hearts. A single voice carries infinite possibilities. Imagine the myriad worlds we can bring into being from one voice.

Additionally, we each carry a unique light language—a language linked to the soul as well as the Origin seed of our family lineage. While this ancient form of expression and connection is not always shared openly, the power are profound. Spoken directly from the soul, light language carries the ability to dissolve old soul contracts and release inherited family patterns—clearing the way for personal and collective healing. This language moves beyond mere words and is often highly tonal, dynamic, and expressive. Learning and speaking our unique light language awakens the unfathomable creative power within our voice and unravels all illusion of separation and reconnects us with the truth of our essence.

Imagine combining your light language with the infinite potential of vocal sound—unstoppable! Unity language and sounds are capable of transforming our inner and outer worlds and carry the power to manifest a new collective reality based in connection, healing, and wholeness. In this emerging paradigm, our voices are no longer seen as tools for communication. Rather, they are understood to be unique vessels for creation and healing aligned with our soul and Unity purpose. Together, we have the power to reshape reality—dissolving the boundaries that once separated us and create new, resonant fields of possibility.

Herbal Insights: Calamus, Hyssop & Sage

☽ **Best Ways to Connect**: Tea | Tincture | Smudging | Infused Oil

🌿 **Calamus** *(Acorus calamus)*
Calamus, known as the herb of eloquence, has been used for millennia to strengthen the voice and enhance clear communication. It supports verbal confidence, making it a powerful ally for public speaking, storytelling, and self-expression. Deeply grounding, Calamus allows words to flow with purpose and clarity, aligning speech with inner wisdom.

🌿 **Hyssop** *(Hyssopus officinalis)*
Hyssop is a herb of purification, traditionally used to clear stagnant emotions that may block communication. It helps open the throat chakra, releasing unspoken words and emotions, allowing for more authentic expression. Whether enjoyed as tea or in aromatherapy, Hyssop encourages courageous and truthful speech while supporting emotional and spiritual clarity.

🌿 **Sage** *(Salvia officinalis)*
Sage is a protector and purifier, known for clearing both physical and energetic blockages. It enhances mental focus and clarity, helping to dispel doubt, confusion, and fear that may inhibit speech. Sage encourages truthful and confident expression, making it a trusted ally for those seeking to speak with wisdom and integrity.

CHAPTER NINE

ANCESTRAL LINEAGE

*OUR LINEAGES WEAVE
THE TAPESTRY OF HUMAN LIFE.*

We are each born into a story—a lineage woven through our family tree. The Origin seed of our lineage holds the truth of why we are here and who we are meant to become. The seed is encoded with intergalactic wisdom, waiting to be fully remembered and understood by the host. Our heritage extends far beyond our immediate family and is rooted in a vast network of ancestors and humanity itself. To truly know ourselves, we must explore not only our individual family history, but the deeper interwoven origins of humanity.

Our journey of self-discovery begins with investigating the beliefs and patterns we carry from childhood. Parents and caregivers can play a significant role in shaping our beliefs. Hopefully the relationship is nurturing: guiding us, keeping us safe, and helping us grow into compassionate and resilient individuals. This manifestation of love is strong and well-meaning, although it can be negatively influenced by the lens of separation—reflecting societal or familial fears and limitations. In the formative years of childhood, our need for validation and acceptance is heightened and shapes how we perceive ourselves and the world at large.

As we look more deeply into the stories of our lineage, we gain insight regarding the roots of our human family and the interconnectedness binding us. By understanding the beliefs and elemental patterns we inherited and revealing the unique wounds of separation our lineage carries, we are able to open ourselves to our soul's Divine purpose and embrace the Unity that transcends all boundaries of time, place, and identity. This journey of remembrance reconnects us with our Origin seed, illuminating the path forward with a sense of wholeness and belonging.

For roughly the past 400 or more years, across countless cultures and ancestral lines, scarcity beliefs have spread like wildfire, forming dominant genetic markers within us. These markers present as elemental lineage patterns that we are born with. Although these markers can be resolved vibrationally, they are often reinforced by statements such as, 'Money doesn't grow on trees,' 'You have to work hard to get by,' or 'There isn't enough to go around.' These beliefs become woven into our sense of self from a young age. Passed down through generations, they create elemental patterns that leave lasting imprints. This is how they become encoded in our genetics, shaping how we live and view the world. It is little wonder we are now facing global crises rooted in division and lack.

Within the illusion of separation, we inherit hidden wisdom—rough diamonds—shaped by the resilience of our ancestors. As we reconnect and embody our soul's lineage, our vibration rises, and these concealed gifts begin to emerge, polished by our awareness, lifting us into our Unity purpose.

Recognizing that these patterns exist within us is a powerful first step, allowing us to acknowledge and begin to transform them. By doing so, we create shifts not only for ourselves but for our entire lineage, paving a path of healing that honors our ancestors and reshapes our family legacy for future generations to come.

Radical forgiveness invites us to extend compassion through every branch of our family tree—reaching seven generations back. In this sacred act, we forgive our parents, grandparents, great-grandparents, and so on, with expansive love and understanding. In recognizing that most wounds are inherited, we are ripe to receive the healing balm of Unity dwelling within the heart. The loving energy of Unity provides a strong foundation for radical forgiveness to take root—healing ourselves and ancestors alike.

As we begin to resolve our generational patterns, we reach a place of acceptance where the past is not forgotten, but rightfully remains in the past and is able to be alchemized. While this may seem like an overly simplified approach to deeply rooted family dynamics, such as abusive behaviors we may have experienced, it is essential to remember that all elemental patterns have the same trajectory—resolution. Remaining stuck in these stories for too long can lead to stagnation, further solidifying the vibrations of past wounds in our bodies. However, we can acknowledge what happened with clarity and courage and find a balance between honoring our experiences and our pain, while not continuing to identify with the past.

Radical forgiveness neither erases nor excuses the past, but transforms the energy, inviting us to step beyond inherited patterns into a space of healing, liberation, and Unity. Through this process, we can both enhance our individual journey and offer our lineage the gift of healing.

As the light of our family diamond begins to shine within us, compassion begins to emerge—shifting the perspective from separation to Unity. In the past emotions were rarely validated and oppression of truth and expression was pervasive, which tragically has been passed down through generations. Despite these challenges, we can learn to honor and thank our ancestors who found ways to shine their light even when their environment likely discouraged it. However, this cyclical pattern is evolving as individuals and the collective begin to expand into Unity.

As we begin the process of remembrance, our purpose—infused with the wisdom of the infinite—starts to unravel within us. There is also a more mysterious dimension of our lineage: our connection to the vast intergalactic realm. We have been genetically re-created with Divine purpose. As our individual Unity purpose begins to bloom, it reflects this divine intention. From this place, we aid the collective's evolutionary leap—we are intimately interconnected, with no separation. Co-creation and growth are our Divine mission. The shift does not happen to us; it takes place within us, guiding us toward the new paradigm.

The Divine essence of the human species is far from a virus destroying the planet. We are here as contributors and protectors of the ecosystem—we are the ecosystem. Just as our bodies are teeming with microbial life, the entity of Earth is covered with and created by animals—ants, whales, and humans alike. And if this sounds crazy, remember this: most of what we have been taught until now has been an illusionary story based in separation. The notion that humans are not part of nature has anthropocentric and biblical origins that enforce the narrative that all of nature is here to serve humans and therefore is at our disposal. Wearing the lens of separation—where humans are not nature—makes it far easier to justify the abobital treatment of Earth and all her creatures.

So what is the truth?

While we are intimately interconnected with Earth, we are not solely of this Earth. A vital piece of human history is missing from the theory of evolution taught in school. The human species did not simply evolve from primates. Many humans feel a deep connection to star nations and ancient civilizations—an intuitive knowing of origin. Feeling "out of place" or a lack of belonging to this planet may indicate being a star seed with an intergalactic purpose. Whether we are conscious of it or not, we carry memories of past lives that span distant dimensions and worlds. These memories are beginning to stir within us for a radical reason.

The story of human creation is interwoven with intergalactic threads. Like all mammals, we play an essential role in Earth's ecosystem, yet we are not quite like other species. Just as

123

every living being on Earth has a unique purpose, so do we—and that purpose includes a cosmic dimension. Our DNA carries the presence of star origins, a unique fusion of earthly and galactic heritage. We are not alone in this connection; dolphins, whales, redwoods, mushrooms, and bees are fellow earthly beings that share this interstellar ancestry. Together, we co-create and contribute to Earth's evolution, each carrying a unique piece of the cosmic puzzle.

The Origin seed of humanity was genetically altered by galactic forces. This is the missing link in the current overculture's understanding of human evolution, for it neglects our Divine purpose. Carrying DNA from a variety of interdimensional beings makes us a unique species on the brink of a great evolutionary leap—leaping into our true nature. Our galactic family co-created humans by merging animal DNA with their own, adding modifications over time.

The roots of our family tree intertwine evolutionary biology with quantum potential, creating a cosmic fusion—Mother Earth and Father Sky. Humans are far more than we have been led to believe. We are a hybrid species with untapped, advanced capabilities. Research in epigenetics reveals that our environment and experiences, including energetic shifts, can activate or deactivate specific genes. This suggests that our DNA holds dormant codes, waiting for the right conditions to be "switched on." For this remembrance to fully awaken, the Unity paradigm's vibration is needed to rise within us.

The intergalactic codes woven into our DNA resonate at such a high frequency that in order to activate these codes our body's vibration must match this frequency. This process parallels the phenomenon of resonance in physics, where two systems vibrate in harmony to amplify each other's power. When our internal vibration reaches this harmonious frequency, our intergalactic heritage awakens within us—paving the way for a profound transformation of consciousness.

Once these codes are activated, they begin to integrate into our cellular structure, creating a profound vibrational alignment. This process engages the neuroplasticity of the brain, allowing us to reshape old patterns, release limiting beliefs, and fully embody the Origin seed of the human species. As the vibrations in our bodies' rise and elemental patterns of separation resovle, we are perfectly poised to embrace our full potential and embody our Divine Unity purpose, allowing our true ancestral lineage to emerge.

As children, play comes naturally. Fully immersed in our imaginations, we explore endless possibilities and an expansive reality. This imaginative play is encouraged at this stage of development for it aligns with our true nature. As we grow older however, we are taught to abandon these parts of ourselves. The dominant culture compels us to conform to a worldview that separates us from our authentic selves. Fortunately, the notion that we can discard our innate imaginative nature is a misconception. The upside-down reality we have been living in—where imagination is suppressed—is beginning to implode within and around us.

Our highly sensitive and attuned bodies are encoded with genetic markers that reinforce behavior. Given much of our conditioning has been guided by separation, our epigenetics tragically and ironically often pull us further and further from the origin seed of Unity planted within us. Neurological patterns related to the fight-flight-freeze response are manipulated by external forces such as media, natural algorithms, and family pressures that reify our imagined fears rooted in past traumas. In turn, we can be directed into actions by fear that perpetuate division.

The key to our evolution lies in activating the Origin seed of our family lineage. Each lineage carries a unique vibrational signature. Through exploring ourselves and our ancestry, we are able to unlock the potential of our Origin seed. This activation not only speeds up our personal growth, but also enhances the evolution of our collective consciousness. We cannot escape our lineage, nor should we. By embracing it, we activate and expand its unique energy. We are directly supported by nurturing our family line—our ancestors near and far—for it feeds our roots, the source of our fullest potential.

Harnessing the condensed energy of our family lineage is foundational to fully embodying and living in Unity.

The ripples of our transformation extend in all directions—seven generations back, in the here and now, and seven generations to come. There is no separation between what we begin to alchemize in ourselves and what begins to shift in our family members. The phenomenon of quantum entanglement in which particles that were once connected remain intertwined regardless of their current distance illustrates how our internal shifts energetically impact people we have close relations with—particularly those in our genetic line. When someone raises their vibration it initiates a subtle, yet powerful transformation across the family line—reshaping ancestral patterns, sparking collective healing.

The first to initiate this transformation within a family is often guided by the soul. This person may be labeled as the black sheep, responding to a call that transcends the physical. Each soul has its own lineage—a soul family that extends beyond biology, united by purpose. Embarking on the journey of investigating and healing our unique conditioning is a deeply spiritual endeavor—one that reconnects us with the ancestral wisdom embedded in our DNA while also addressing the unhealed wounds passed down through generations.

As we begin this potent process, family members may perceive us as unstable or overly sensitive. It is important we see these perceptions and projections clearly as stemming from people not yet able to understand and support the layers we are

126

unearthing. This misinterpretation is often a reflection of their own unresolved emotions and conditioning.

Those who step forward are the torchbearers—moving through the dense and often uncharted terrain of family wounds, clearing the way for others.

Throughout our many lives we have been both the perpetrator & the victim. This understanding eliminates the need to identify scapegoats—in our family or elsewhere—and breeds boundless compassion.

Being born into a family modeling and teaching scarcity-based beliefs can make us feel stuck, leading to blame and complacency as if others are responsible for our limitations. This mindset blocks energy flow and perpetuates fear-based patterns that keep us from our true potential. While survival matters, we do not have to make soul compromises! We can find true safety and abundance without sacrificing our Unity purpose.

In compassionate communities and meaningful relationships, we can find support to grow beyond these patterns and lay the foundation for new ways. As our vibration evolves, we often connect with people who quickly become an adopted family that guide us through our transformation. Self-compassion and forgiveness are essential to keeping our energy clear as we wade through the mud. Creating distance from our family can help us reach a place of neutrality and understanding that ultimately supports our familial reunion when the time is right.

We are all fragments of Divine light, unified by eternal love. All illusions of separation stem from

*skewed perception and obscure the underlying Unity
that connects us & lives within us.*

*Bless our family lineages & the Origin seed of love
that each family tree grew from.*

Family voice

The harmonics of our family's spoken words create a unique resonance, distinguishing one family from another. Lineages remain interconnected through the language used. Words carry great weight and thus can either further Unity or separation. When we consciously choose to speak affirmations of love and acceptance, a profound resonance occurs between family members. This loving vibration touches whoever is connected, even if they are not physically present where the words are shared.

By intentionally speaking affirmations we tap into this sacred phenomenon, both tending to our present day relations and stoking our ancestral connections. As we speak words of healing, love, and transformation, we create a resonant field that reaches into the past and the future, while also suffusing the present. This practice has the potential to bring about profound shifts within ourselves and our ancestral lineage—fostering healing and empowering new narratives to unfold.

Transformational affirmations help rewrite ancestral lineage. Remember the power of speaking aloud, for the act of forming words creates vibration and thus reifies the affirmation we speak. Beyond these examples, explore creating personal affirmations!

"I release inherited patterns that no longer serve my highest good. I am creating a new path of empowerment and love for myself and future generations."

"I call on the inherent love that has seeded my family tree, recognize the love within my family. I choose love for myself and my family. I embrace my innate power to shape my destiny and create a positive legacy."

"I choose love and compassion as the guiding principles in my life, transcending the judgments and scars of the past. I am creating a new paradigm of healing and growth for myself and my family."

"I forgive and release any ancestral wounds, allowing healing and transformation to flow through me. I am a vessel of love, carrying forward the wisdom and strength of my ancestors."

"I embrace my unique purpose and gifts. I am untethered by the constraints of outdated ancestral beliefs. I am rewriting the story of my ancestral lineage—creating a legacy of love, authenticity, fulfillment, and Unity."

Repetition is required to establish new patterns.... a pattern only becomes a pattern through repetition. So, repeat these affirmations (or your own) often!

Herbal Insights: Mugwort, Rosemary & Palo Santo

☽ **Best Ways to Connect**: Tea | Incense | Infused Oil | Ritual Work

🌿 **Mugwort** *(Artemisia vulgaris)*
Mugwort is a revered herb in shamanic traditions, known for enhancing dreams, intuition, and ancestral connection. She is one of the most compassionate plant allies, and chances are, you are already under her protective presence. Acting as a bridge between the physical and spiritual realms, Mugwort supports dream work, divination, and deep introspection. She clears energetic blockages and reveals hidden truths, guiding us toward greater self-awareness and clarity.

🌿 **Ways to Connect**: Drink as tea before sleep to enhance dreams, burn as incense for ritual work, or place under a pillow for dream recall.

🌿 **Rosemary** *(Salvia rosmarinus)*
Rosemary is a sacred herb of remembrance, protection, and clarity. Used throughout history to honor ancestors, she strengthens memory and insight while clearing stagnant energy from the mind and space. Rosemary supports clear thinking and fortifies personal energy, making her a trusted ally for those seeking guidance from the past or clarity for the future.

🌿 **Ways to Connect**: Burn dried rosemary to purify a space, steep in tea for mental clarity, or anoint with rosemary-infused oil to enhance focus and intuition.

CHAPTER TEN

WE ARE NOT ALONE

AWAKENING TO THE UNSEEN: COMMUNING WITH
GUIDES, THE UNIVERSAL MIND, AND NATURE

Explaining our awakening experiences to others can be draining, especially when words cannot fully capture what we are going through. Much of what we believed in is now falling away from us.The Unity vibration we hold is not always relatable to those friends and family that we relied upon in the past to confide in.

Taking time away from others is a gentle way to rest and reconnect with the spaciousness within, giving the body space to adjust to its vibrational shift. It's important to remember that solitude is not synonymous with loneliness. If being alone feels uncomfortable, that discomfort is an invitation to face it. For many, extended periods of solitude can bring unease. In these moments, the absence of external distractions forces us to confront our inner landscape and thoughts rooted in separation.

The habitual patterns and programming sustained by the constant influx of survival- and fear-based messages begin to dissolve when we are alone. This process, though liberating, can feel unsettling. Without the usual distractions, we come face-to-face with these thoughts and begin to see them for what they are—illusions.

The experience of being alone varies for everyone, shaped by factors such as how often we've practiced solitude, its duration, and how much we've already resolved beliefs tied to separation. We can ease into solitude with incremental steps: perhaps starting with a half-hour, then an hour, and eventually spending an entire day immersed in nature or quietly at home—without speaking, scrolling, or engaging with the outside world.

As the mental chatter softens, a sense of Remembrance begins to unfurl within. This is the Remembrance of Unity, a profound realization that we are never truly alone. Paradoxically, this understanding often emerges most deeply through physical solitude. The very etymology of "alone"—derived from "all one"—offers a quiet hint at this truth.

The phrase "We are never alone" carries profound implications. Depending on our belief structure, it may refer to the presence of Beings of Light, ancestral guides, and animal or plant allies. It also reminds us of the most vital guide of all—ourselves—and our innate ability to connect with the all-knowing neutrality of love—Universal Mind.

This is the space where illusions dissolve, leaving only truth. While this understanding is not new, it remains timeless. Meditation, often described as the art of being alone, offers us a pathway to this realization. All great masters throughout history have attained enlightenment through the practice of solitude and self-reflection.

Do you have experiences of seeing, feeling, or hearing guides that exist in the subtle, unseen realms? Perhaps you've sensed a presence beyond the physical—a whisper of intuition, a quiet knowing, or an unexplainable feeling of support. These guides, though often invisible, can make themselves known in delicate and personal ways. Can you open your heart and mind to the possibility that such guidance is real and ever-present, waiting for you to notice?

Can you believe such guidance is even possible? To trust in the unseen is an act of faith, requiring a willingness to explore beyond the limits of the physical world. It invites us to consider the presence of something greater—a gentle force that weaves through our experiences, offering insight and reassurance.

Have you ever felt drawn toward the idea of unseen guidance that quietly shapes your path, even if it cannot be easily explained?

When was the last time you were completely alone, with no external devices or distractions? Think back to the last moment you truly stepped away from the noise of modern life. No phone in hand, no screens pulling your attention, no demands on your time—just you and the quiet presence of your own company. How often do we grant ourselves such moments? In a world buzzing with distractions, true solitude becomes a gift we rarely open.

How does it feel when you are all alone? What emotions come to the surface when there is no one else around, nothing to distract you from yourself? Is there a sense of peace, or does discomfort bubble up?

Perhaps you feel both—a sense of grounding mixed with a longing or unease. Whatever arises, sitting with those feelings can be a doorway to understanding yourself on a deeper level. Solitude has a way of revealing the emotions we often keep tucked away.

How does it feel right now just thinking about being completely alone? Close your eyes and imagine yourself in that space, with nothing but your breath and thoughts for company. Does the idea feel liberating or intimidating—or maybe a little of both? This reflection, even in thought, invites you to explore your relationship with solitude and the emotions it awakens. Within that exploration lies an opportunity to meet yourself fully, in the stillness and silence of being.

Solitude is a wonderful way to sort things out. In the peace of our own company, deep wells of wisdom and understanding are revealed. Seeking and doing less—the act of surrendering—is often the best and strongest medicine.

The current dominant culture places little value on being alone, slowing down, or simply doing nothing. In fact, society is structured to resist and even suppress these fundamental needs, often dismissing or judging those who choose to honor the quiet call that arises from within. This criticism, rooted in ignorance, reflects a culture that prioritizes constant productivity over the well-being of the soul.

We are typically only encouraged to slow down and let go at the very end of life's race—retirement—when our energy has often been depleted by years of relentless striving. But what if taking time alone and embracing moments of stillness were among the most productive things we could do? Such practices offer space for reflection, healing, and alignment with our true nature, creating a foundation for greater balance and clarity.

In the Unity paradigm, periods of rest and doing less will not only be normalized but also celebrated and encouraged. These moments of pause will no longer be seen as indulgent or wasteful but as essential parts of living a harmonious life. By embracing stillness, we create the opportunity to reconnect with ourselves, each other, and the natural rhythms that guide all living things.

If we believe it is impossible to step away from everything for three days—or even a month—we may be caught in the grip of egoic scarcity beliefs. This mindset convinces us that there is never enough time, that life demands constant action, and that pausing is a luxury we cannot afford. If we fear that everything will crumble simply because we take time to be alone, it may be a sign that our lives are deeply entangled in the illusion of separation.

And if that fear proves true—if our world does indeed collapse because we choose to honor our inner need to reset—then perhaps it is time to let it fall apart.

What is worth clinging to in a system that cannot accommodate our most fundamental needs? By releasing the broken structures, we create space for something new and more aligned to emerge.

For if we have built a reality that does not allow for retreat or renewal, then we can be certain of one thing: when powerful vibrational shifts inevitably occur, that reality will fall apart. It is not a question of if but of when. Recognizing this truth invites us to begin letting go on our terms, creating the conditions for transformation before it is forced upon us.

Unity Belief
"We can leave, and we can come back."

Many of us have reached a point in our lives where it no longer makes sense to continue as we always have. We are hungry and desperate for change. Compelled to take a leap into the unknown, we are supported by the Divine. The writing is on the wall and we feel it in our bones—we need to be alone. Can we honor the call?

The length of this solitary experience differs person to person—not everyone needs to commit to a month-long retreat. However, three days tends to be the minimum length we need. Find an environment that supports winding down, down regulating the nervous system. Maybe it's an intentional "stay-cation" where we cut the cord to all external devices to help deprogram the body. Maybe we leave town for a few days—rent a spot or camp out.

136

Let's not beat around the bush: when our lives begin to unravel because we no longer embody the separation beliefs that once gave us a false sense of reality, the experience of being alone changes profoundly. In these moments, when we have lost all sense of self, and the ego can no longer pretend to be in control, we may find ourselves alone—not by choice, but by circumstance. This aloneness brings us face-to-face with a deeply systemic fear that lives in the body, often translating into a terrifying experience.

For those who have entered the unknown in this way, the depth of grief and excruciating pain is all too familiar. It is an experience we would wish upon no one, yet it remains an undeniable part of the journey back to Unity. These pivotal times, though painful, are markers of transformation. They arise from time to time as we move through chaotic nodes of frequency shifts, requiring ascension skills to navigate.

In these moments, the art of neutrality becomes a lifeline. Fear may manifest as intense thoughts, physical pain, or relentless self-judgment, but by anchoring ourselves in the neutrality of love, we learn to sit with these emotions, even when they feel as far from the light as imaginable. This process, though deeply uncomfortable, is not fatal. With each breath, as we allow the purging to unfold, we birth a new way of being.

From this rebirth comes clarity. Thoughts become more coherent, energy begins to flow, and the sense of disorder—of entropy—begins to diminish. In this renewed state, we are reminded of the intimately interwoven and interconnected reality we are part of. The boundless, eternal source of love begins to infuse our system, re-establishing our unique connection to the love that has always lived within us.

It is truly remarkable how, in this space, we can feel less alone while being physically alone. In fact, solitude often feels far less isolating than being surrounded by others in a world governed by separation. In this realization, we reconnect with the truth of our Unity and the infinite love that sustains us.

When we finally enter into the unknown and trust its remarkable intelligence and innate safety we can experience awakening moments that change us forever.

How are you practicing and preparing going into the unknown?

Once we move beyond the chaotic node, we begin to embody the incremental frequency shift. The vibration we now hold allows the nervous system to rest and heal from the constant onslaught of repetitive, fear-based noise that reinforces stories of separation. However, maintaining this high vibration can be challenging, as deeply ingrained reactions often become addictive for the body; they are like deep ruts. Yet, each time we shift the body's vibration, these ruts become smaller, making it easier to move out of them. Unfortunately, we often stick to familiar paths, even if they are not the best, because the unknown can feel riskier. For instance, our shadow can act like a drug. We may become dependent on the negative feedback loops that trigger specific reactions, flooding the body with chemicals such as cortisol, norepinephrine, adrenaline, glutamate, and dopamine (often spiked by using electronic devices). These well-known mental patterns and biochemical releases contribute to the discomfort of being alone for extended periods. In essence, we are experiencing withdrawal symptoms.

Just like with any addiction, we must face some discomfort as we work through it. This discomfort lessens each time we reaffirm our commitment to returning to our true nature and living in alignment with our purpose.

What feels frightening about being alone or stepping away from our responsibilities? Can you imagine letting everything go—your job, your house, your relationships? From this place, what does it feel like?

Could it be that deep down, we sense that if we take this time to be alone and begin to resolve the separation patterns of our life, those patterns—and our life as we know it—might completely transform?

It can be supportive to explore skillful ways to cope and stoke our sense of interconnection. For instance, spreading time outside can help ease the transition from the busy human world by being surrounded by the dynamic natural world.

Fortunately the present moment makes it significantly easier to maintain higher vibrations in the body. What once took years to achieve can now happen more swiftly and with greater ease due to growing awareness and awakening in the collective. By unplugging for at least three days, we allow the emerging Unity paradigm within us to take root and reset our system. It is like restarting the computer for an updated software to be installed. Times of quietude are necessary to learn and integrate the new. By embracing solitude we accelerate the resolution of separation beliefs and elemental patterns. We are lovingly led to our birthright of profound bliss.

In the sacred space of solitude we are often gifted great insights that can take a variety of forms. As energy flows increase within the body, additional insights into our true nature are revealed and the soul opens to receive communication from life in new, foreign feeling ways. Let us delve into this delicate territory with the utmost care and intention. When the whispers of the subtle realms or the voice of our higher selves touch our ears, mind, or heart we embark on the journey of discernment. Amidst the labyrinth of the mind, we learn the difference between internal messages rooted in fear and Unity-based messages that reflect our Divinity.

Cultivating the art of discernment—distinguishing between projections of the mind and authentic inner communication—requires presence, practice, and patience. Take the time to feel the difference. When we spend time alone, we can begin to clear the separation filters that may distort authentic inner knowing. Being alone helps establish pathways for deeper trust. We start to recognize the difference between true authentic inner knowing and the survival mechanisms of the body and mind.

Everyone's communication skills manifest differently at first. For some, it's a feeling; for others, it's visual or a thought; and for some, it's auditory. We begin where we are. The language of our inner knowing is individual and sacred.

However, processing these threads of information can be influenced by the shadowy parts of ourselves that still exist in separation. The way we interpret these flows of information can be subjective. For this reason, learning the language of the subtle realms, as the messages and information we receive are often cloaked in codes and symbolism. They are not always meant to be taken literally. Tread carefully along the tightrope that separates genuine communication from the illusions of delusion.

Unity belief
I trust that I can communicate with my Divinity

These sacred, unseen relationships are unique to each one of us. As the flows of love increase, integrating these energies becomes second nature. There's nothing to fear as we continuously fine-tune our engagement with our divinity, we open conscious pathways to the Universal Mind that is the doorway to the quantum field and all dimensions. And in its purest sense how we are creating timelines in our lives,

When we spend time alone, we may notice that the messages we receive become increasingly magnified and deeply connected to our Unity purpose, guiding us toward precise and intentional action. In the stillness of solitude and the neutrality of love, we hold a Unity vibration that opens the way for clear and authentic guidance. By honoring this information and acting on it in real-world situations, we often find ourselves stepping into the unknown. However, the power of trusting in rightful action—and the divinely inspired messages from the Universal Mind—reveals that our steps have already been anticipated. Inspired connections will meet us along the way, leading to the next aligned action. For this reason, taking action is essential. Yet the beauty of that action often begins with simply being alone, deeply listening, and trusting what unfolds.

Unity Belief
I completely trust my inner knowing.

Deepening the relationship and trust with our inner knowing, and awakening dormant parts of ourselves, is how we begin to cultivate a unified relationship with our Divinity. This is why being alone is so important. The space created while being alone serves as a blank canvas for a new inner landscape to be painted.

Yes, we are the artists of this new inner landscape, one that is in harmony with our true nature. We are the ones who co-create our reality in Unity. We do not allow anyone else to do that for us. We develop trust in our super-intelligent nature, feeling the interconnectedness beyond mere intellectualization. We realize that we possess one of the most sophisticated natural operating systems on the planet.

Is believing seeing, or is seeing believing? The unseen realms remain hidden for now, but soon, everyone will start experiencing a heightened sense of inner knowing. From this place, we can confidently deepen our connection with ascended masters, guides, plants, animals, the elements, ancestors, extraterrestrial beings, the winged ones, and our higher self. All of this is possible because it's within us. As we begin to trust the biofield that surrounds and sustains us, we realize that we are the quantum field itself. We are divine co-creators, inseparable from the creator, because we are creators.

Yes, we can create relationships with any of these beings and become good friends with them. It is the same as any other relationship: a sharing of energy and information in union.

It's fun and exciting. There is no race to be won, no competition to claim victory. Feelings, perceptions, and receptions of communication are as varied as the tapestry of existence itself. Everyone is capable of communicating with the subtle realms. It may present as a feeling, a bird arriving on a stoop, a dream, or even a seemingly out-of-place thought. A line in a song at the right time can be a message. Do not compare your way of communicating to others, and do not believe there is only one way, as it is always evolving. A method that appeared once may never appear that way again.

The importance of being receptive to these communications and believing they are real is all that is required. This openness makes life expansive and fulfilling. We are not alone, and we don't have to figure everything out. We are in a relationship with the multiverse and have access to everything the divine has ever created.

We do not aim to declare one way superior to another. Instead, we extend an earnest invitation—a gentle call—to unlock the doors of our being, forging relationships with dormant aspects within. It is in this dance of discovery that pleasure and joy unfurl, as we traverse the subtle realms and revel in the comforting truth that we are never truly alone.

Connecting with your guides:

Find a quiet space, free from distractions. Sit or lie down comfortably, and let your body settle into a state of ease. Close your eyes and take a deep breath, allowing the air to fill your lungs.

In the stillness, let your mind relax and your thoughts subside. Imagine yourself standing at the edge of a vast, shimmering lake, its surface reflecting the hues of the sky above.

Feel the gentle breeze brushing against your skin, carrying whispers from the subtle realms. Listen closely to the rustle of leaves and the distant calls of birds as nature's symphony weaves around you.

With each breath, envision a golden light emanating from within, expanding and enveloping your entire being. This radiant light serves as a beacon, inviting your spirit guides to draw near.

In this tranquil space, invite your guides to reveal themselves in a form that resonates with you—be it an animal, an angelic presence, or a wise ancestral figure. Trust that they will manifest in a way that speaks to your heart.

As you open your senses to their presence, engage in silent conversation. Speak from the depths of your soul, expressing your intentions, questions, or desires. Allow space for their responses to gently arise within you—be it in words, feelings, or intuitive knowing.

Absorb their wisdom and guidance with reverence, letting it infuse every fiber of your being. Embrace their insights and messages as gifts from the subtle realms.

When you feel ready, express gratitude to your guides for their presence and guidance. Slowly bring your awareness back to the present moment, feeling the support of the ground beneath you. Take a deep breath, exhaling any remaining tension or doubts.

Carry the essence of this connection with you as you navigate your days. Know that the lines of communication with the subtle realms and your spirit guides remain open, ready to guide and inspire you.

As you gently open your eyes, let the serenity of this meditation linger, and step forward with renewed purpose and connection to the expansive tapestry of existence.

Herbal Insights: Lily & Angelica

☽ **Best Ways to Connect:** Tea | Tincture | Infused Oil | Spiritual Offering

🌸 **Lily** *(Lilium spp.)*
Lily is a flower of divine purity, grace, and renewal. Revered across spiritual traditions, she carries the essence of angelic presence and higher consciousness. Her soft yet radiant energy cleanses the spirit, offering emotional healing and inner peace. Lily is known to open the heart, release stagnant grief, and invite divine blessings. In dreamwork and meditation, she brings clarity and gentle guidance from the unseen realms.

☽ **Ways to Connect:** Place fresh lilies in sacred spaces for cleansing | Use lily-infused oil for emotional healing | Meditate with the flower to invite angelic insight

🌿 **Angelica** *(Angelica archangelica)*
Angelica, often called the Herb of the Angels, is a powerful ally for protection, spiritual connection, and strength. Named after the Archangels, she has long been regarded as a divine gift for healing and guidance. Angelica clears negative energy, strengthens intuition, and provides grounded spiritual protection. Used in ritual baths, incense, and teas, she enhances connection with angelic beings and inner wisdom.

☽ **Ways to Connect:** Burn dried angelica for purification | Steep as tea for inner strength | Carry as a talisman for protection and guidance

CHAPTER ELEVEN

SHADOW

*WE ARE NOT OUR SHADOW. AND YET, WE ARE NEVER
WITHOUT IT. FOREVER ACCOMPANYING US,
WE LEARN TO SEE IT CLEARLY. IN TIME, WE GROW
BEYOND THE SHAPE ON THE GROUND.*

The shadow is the muddled, misunderstood, and wounded part of ourselves. The unacknowledged shadow projects its fears—namely not belonging to the world—into the crevasses of our lives. The shadow keeps appearing until it has been loved. Any attempt to pretend it does not exist only exacerbates the shadow's sense of being neglected, delaying the inevitable resurfacing of the wounded, splintered inner child. The shadow tries to keep us safe by using exaggerated separation beliefs based in fear.

The child simply wants to be in a
loving relationship with everything and everyone.
Our true nature is to be curious, creative, loving,
imaginative, & intimately connected with the natural world.

A person's shadow self is largely created by living in a separation paradigm, distinct from our childhood experiences—our true nature. Childhood conditioning, family lineage, recent trauma, and unresolved past-life trauma can also contribute to the development of a shadow self.

When relationships malfunction in our lives, we often perceive these fractures to be external events happening "to us." Our inner shadow internalizes these fractures, viewing them as evidence of the insatiable darkness that is intent on perpetuating our suffering. However, this darkness is merely a reflection of the separation within us. In reality, it is an illusion—a shadow obscuring the light that is always within us. The shadow thrives on feelings of disempowerment and hopelessness, since these emotions are connected to the wounded ego and lack of validation. The shadow often projects its perceived pain in the way of anger, blame, and judgment.

The fundamental belief "I am not safe" comes into play here, indicating the emergence of our shadow. The embodiment and internalization of belief patterns is a survival mechanism that reappears throughout our lives desperately wanting to be resolved.

When we shift our reactions into responses—seeing each moment as a lesson—the shadow begins–to diminish.

The departure from our natural state of Unity generates a splintered, parallel reality. In an effort to heal this imbalance and resolve the illusion of separation, the body and psyche establish new elemental patterns with the Origin seed of Unity. This gives rise to the shadow—creating sub-personalities that are designed to keep us safe.

As we grow up and attend school, we undergo socialization—modifying our behavior to fit into various societal norms and groups. Some individuals find this process more easeful than others. The education system perpetuates the indoctrination of the separation paradigm, reinforcing the belief that we are *separate* from our inner knowing, nature, and bodies. This divide leads to an increased reliance on external systems for survival since our trust in our highly intelligent guidance systems and innate knowledge has been undermined.

Deep within each of us lies a shadow self, characterized by surface-level interactions that block meaningful connections. This shadow is fed by illusion—the vital force that sustains its existence. We all have shadows, though they may vary in intensity. When overly nourished, the shadow can become a destructive force, leading to personalities marked by manipulation, greed, envy, violence, and self-absorption. This distorted illusion of separation manifests through paranoid, violent language and, at times, physical violence. It thrives on keeping us disconnected from our true selves, preventing us from feeling safe or powerful.

Though the shadow may present the illusion of being in right relationship, it is not. It acts against our best interests, perpetuating a painful and isolating existence for those who struggle to build a genuine connection with all parts of themselves. The question is: can we learn to care for our shadow, offering it the love and validation it so desperately craves, while dismantling the illusion that sustains its power? By doing so, we can integrate the shadow into a part of ourselves that supports, rather than hinders, our wholeness.

Exaggerated separation beliefs create a dense vibration in the body. This heaviness creates stagnant energy and becomes the shadow.

There is no separation between the individual shadow and the collective shadow—one creates the other and vice versa. This is how shadows spread, perpetuate separation beliefs, and create convoluted realities that further wound and oppress the masses.

Just as the shadow spreads, the Unity vibration is spreading within us and between us—shining healing light on the shadowy parts of ourselves and our culture.

When a radiant child possesses an old soul, their brilliance can attract deeply wounded individuals. These hurt individuals unconsciously yearn to reconnect with the eternal state of love and purity; however, it can manifest in twisted and unjust ways such as harming the child through sexaul-abuse or violence. As a result, children with ancient souls often endure the most profound traumas.

At the moment of trauma, these souls may split and hover above the body, creating a feeling of not belonging and therefore reinforcing separation beliefs. At the same time, this experience can foster a profound connection with the Divine—opening new pathways to resolve the separation patterns born from the traumatic event. These children have a unique and soul purpose.

This complex phenomenon has given rise to many wounded healers. From the soul's perspective, enduring suffering serves a higher purpose—it allows for resolution and helps others heal from patterns of separation. As individuals embark on their journey toward Unity, the reunification of the fragmented soul with the body accelerates the awakening process. To the amazement of many, even individuals facing homelessness or addiction might experience a profound spiritual awakening in the early stages of ascension. We are all Divine and worthy of awakening. There is no separation!

Let's pause and center ourselves.
Inhale Love, exhale Gratitude.
Imagine reuniting with your inner child.
Take a moment to love that child—maybe a tender hug,
laughter, reliving a prized memory...
whatever calls you most.

When we engage with dark realities through discussions, literature, or media we are reminded of our own potential for darkness, its unavoidable nature, and the impact it can have on those we care about. By shedding light on the underlying causes of these harsh realities, we demystify them and gain a deeper understanding as to why dark behaviors occur within the human species. Distorted thoughts of separation reinforce this dark and fearful reality and simultaneously reify the shadow within. The vibrations that continually emanate from this mindstate keeps us locked into the old paradigm, sustaining the illusion of separation.

We are not at war with these energies—we create them. To dispel heavy shadow energy, we need to stop feeding the illusion, which begins with an inner investigation.

What demons of division currently live within you?

How does your shadow appear in your relationships?

What is one way your shadow emerged today?

When observing the miracle of nature, we will not see evil in the ecosystem. So, why are evil forces present in the human species? If we believe evil exists and subscribe to narratives of good and bad, heaven and hell, we stoke the veil of evil in our lives. Whatever we believe in, we actively look for. We are programmed to seek confirmation of our beliefs. When this belief is alive within us it generates fear and leads to violence. All of this reinforces the foundational belief, fear belief "I am not safe."

Unity Belief
Evil is an Illusion

The invitation is to say this phrase aloud with an emphasis on *illusion*. How does it feel in the body? Can you notice a distinct vibration emerge or a unique sensation? Possibly one of softening or resting back into the truth of safety?

The shadow is not who we truly are, as individuals or as a species. We have been tormented, oppressed, and traumatized into believing we are inherently evil, violent, or greedy. Nothing could be further from the truth—our real nature is compassionate, loving, expansive, and creative. Yet, the shadow encourages us to fulfill these false prophecies, clouded by the thick lens of separation.

The shadow thrives on avoidance and shallow emotions, preventing us from forming meaningful connections that allow raw and vulnerable feelings to emerge that clear blocked energy.

Becoming aware of how we think, speak, and act toward ourselves helps us begin to witness the reality we are creating in the external world. In moments of disempowerment and self-judgment, we feed our shadow. The hidden little secrets in our inner landscape, known only to ourselves and often concealed by shame, constitute the realm of the shadow.

The most powerful way to witness the shadow is by entering the neutrality of love. Instead of feeling shame about distorted thoughts, we can express gratitude for the opportunity to see them through the lens of neutrality and gratitude. There is nothing to fear.

The Shadow would have us believe that it is others who are at fault for our lives not being whole or abundant. It's not me. *It's not my fault.* These shadowed thoughts manifest as blame and judgment, projecting our wounds onto others. It could be a partner, a coworker, or the government—as long as we avoid taking responsibility for the illusion and our own personal wounds, we feel safe. But this false sense of security creates division, draining our energy and power.

As we confront and witness the dark illusion of the shadow, feelings of hopelessness and grief may emerge, making it feel impossible to escape and overcome. We search for relief in any way we can. These times are not fatal, although it may feel as such. It is best to become a witness and ride the waves trusting the law of impermanence. The excruciating pain we feel in the heart space is part of the healing process. Poignantly, is where the shadow excels and can exert its power. It wants us to believe we are not okay and cannot survive without its "protection." The shadow is the manifestation of the separation paradigm—its ugly illusions and reflections of darkness keep us stuck. As we resolve separation beliefs, we can see our shadow behaviors in a new light.

We try to pull ourselves out of repetitive dark thoughts, but they keep pulling us back in. In those moments, it is hard not to believe they are true, for they are painfully convincing.

Unity Belief
I can love the darkness into light.

Here is a list of natural remedies that can help increase energy flows, open the heart, and ease our experience of pain:

- Ceremonial Cacao
- Blue Lotus
- Blue Vervain Tincture
- Psilocybin, Hero dose or (microdosed)
- Rose Essential Oil
- Tulsi Tea

The shadow finds myriad ways to infiltrate our lives—all in the name of "protection."

Projection: Attributing our undesirable traits or emotions onto others. For example, blaming others for the anger and scarcity we experience, "It's their fault I'm this way."

Overreaction: Having an emotional response that is disproportionately intense compared to the situation. For instance, feeling extreme anger over minor annoyances.

Triggers: During the vibrational shift, we may experience more frequent emotional triggers as we begin to actively resolve patterns of separation.

Self-Sabotage: Allowing the shadow to lead, fearing our own power and potential for growth.

Addictive Behaviors: Using addiction to avoid facing painful aspects of the self, to self soothe, and feel connected to ourselves.

Separation Patterns: Repeatedly finding oneself in similar negative situations, such as consistently entering and staying in unhealthy relationships.

Internal Conflicts: Feeling torn between the separation paradigm and the Unity paradigm, leading to confusion and indecision.

Defensiveness: Reacting defensively can showcase separation beliefs. Pay attention as defensive behaviors increase, as they indicate areas needing resolution.

Criticism and Judgment: Harshly criticizing or judging others, especially for traits or behaviors that one possesses, but has not yet found ways to love or alchemize.

Within the realm of shadow, secrecy and shame flourish The ego thrives when we conceal our challenges and protect ourselves with hushed whispers. Feelings of marginalization and disempowerment are often skillfully hidden behind a meticulously crafted facade of normalcy. Vulnerability, authenticity, and sadness are rejected and pushed into the Shadow—the back dusty corner of the heart. These truths are then covered over by a forced cheer, masking our inner turmoil. Retreating into insignificance becomes the norm, a tragic demonstration of the human spirit's struggle for recognition and belonging.

The Unity vibration is nourished by vulnerability and honesty. It recognizes the futility of pretending everything is fine when it is not. The genuine and unfiltered love flowing through us exposes how we have concealed the pain of separation and the related consequences. Realizing this Unity truth initiates a transformative shift in our understanding of ourselves and our relationships.

Unity Belief
I see you child. And I love all of you.

Much of our Shadow is created when we are a child. As children we are sponges and are subject to influences from parents, caregivers, teachers, and media. Our adult models have an immense impact on our orientation to and experience of life—forming our values, establishing our internal navigation systems, shaping the degree and flavor of shadow we inherit, and more.

As children, we desperately crave validation and love from our caregivers, which in turn shapes our sense of self (i.e., do we feel seen, worthy, valued, etc.). Rooted in survival, we instinctively alter ourselves to ensure we win their affection, gain approval, or receive attention. In doing so we often absorb the beliefs, behaviors, and patterns they model. While these learned dynamics may foster connection, they can also instill habits of separation within us. For instance, we may subtly distance ourselves from authenticity to fit their expectations.

The mother-father-child relationship is foundational, directly influencing how we navigate relationships as adults. The ability to express needs, offer love, and set boundaries is often based on the formation of these patterns early in life. If a caregiver's love felt conditional, we might adopt behaviors such as people-pleasing, withholding emotions, or seeking control in hopes of maintaining the connection.

When Shadows emerge, they reflect the unmet needs or unprocessed emotions we have carried since childhood. For example, if we learned that manipulation was the safest way to secure affection or that expressing emotions led to rejection, we might subconsciously perpetuate these patterns in adulthood for it is what we know. These Shadows can obscure our authentic selves, making it challenging to live in alignment. For instance, we may yearn for love, but through self-sabotage—a frequent manifestation of Shadow energy—prevent the flourishing of love in our life for we fear vulnerability and intimacy.

By exploring our early imprints, we begin to untangle learned behavior from our innate essence of love and our boundless capacity for connection. Recognizing where the shadows dwell allows us to bring light and awareness to the ways we communicate and share our emotional truths.

Parenting in today's world carries profound challenges. Parents navigate the inherent demands of raising children while simultaneously carrying the weight of their lineage and the collective energy of humanity. While this responsibility can feel immense, it also offers opportunities for great healing and transformation. Unconditional love—the binding force of all existence—becomes the light that guides us. It has the power to bridge the deepest fractures and dissolve separation.

The love between a parent and child is sacred. When that bond is honored, it nurtures a foundation of safety, trust, and connection. However, when it is neglected or broken, the shadow arises—not as an enemy, but as a survival mechanism to protect the vulnerable child. Although the integrity of the bond may be weakened, the bond remains intact when fractures occur. The belief, "I am not safe," the fundamental belief of the separation paradigm is reinforced and manifests as Shadow. When the shadow is not seen and resolved, it is passed on through generations.

Given the nature of the separation paradigm, our innate wisdom and Divine essence may often feel in conflict with our inherited beliefs and behaviors and the external world. As infants, we are akin to delicate sprouts—absorbing life's lessons with a raw openness. While each experience certainly shapes us, we arrive with the wisdom of the universe encoded within us. At birth, we are whole, not yet tainted by separation or shadow. However, the environment we live in often imposes structures and beliefs that cloud this purity, dimming the light of our universal knowing.

The reality is the vibration of the human collective instantly begins to vibrationally entrain the infant into the illusion of separation.

As humanity shifts toward a Unity paradigm, the potential exists for children to be born free of these inherited shadows. In this new reality, children will no longer carry beliefs of separation and solely embody the wholeness of their Divine true nature. Until that time, we are the ones tasked with learning and re-learning how to love—not only our children and each other, but also the wounded parts of ourselves. Wonderfully, it is never too late to extend love to the inner child within us who most likely has felt neglected and misunderstood.

Many of us have experienced moments when our bright inner light was unduly dimmed by separation energy such as fear or rejection. The essence of this light however remains intact and patiently waits to be rekindled, for our inner fire can never be entirely extinguished. Through compassion and awareness, we can repair the threads of connection within ourselves and with others, thereby creating a world where the cycle of separation ends. Each act of love—toward our children, our inner child, or each other—brings us closer to the Unity we are destined to return to.

Take a moment to pause and reflect on a time when your light felt dimmed. Do you remember an instance as a child where you felt unseen or mistreated? Recalling these moments, though painful, can offer a profound opportunity for healing.

The practice begins by sitting with the emotion—allowing the feelings to emerge from the memory and flood the body. Then as the wise adults that we are, we hold our current self, our child self, and the memory itself with a tender neutrality, offering all parts unconditional love and compassion. We are able to "reparent" these wounded parts of ourselves by creating a space for our inner child to feel both acknowledged and safe to express their truth—their emotions—without consequences or judgment.

Visualize yourself as a child. Picture your small face, your tender heart, and innocence in your eyes. Imagine opening your arms wide and lovingly embracing this child. Hold yourself with compassion and tenderness, allowing the love you extend to wash away the loneliness or pain that may be present for your younger self. Feel the emotions—not to relive the story and further salt your wounds—but to acknowledge what you felt in those painful moments, alchemizing hurt into healing.

In this sacred space of deeper understanding, grieving and sadness may arise. Whatever emerges is fully welcomed, for these parts create the whole of who you are. These emotions, born from unmet needs or moments of disconnection, are pathways to resolution of elemental patterns. When we sit with these emotions through the lens of love, the patterns they created are softened into transformation.

Through this potent practice, we prepare ourselves to love in ways we may have once thought were unimaginable. We reclaim the parts of ourselves that felt lost, unworthy, or forgotten, birthing Unity within us. The separation that began as an Origin seed in childhood is now met with the radiant light of compassion, dissolving the illusion that we are anything but whole.

Inner child work is transformative and cannot be bypassed. It takes us to the Origin—the point where the seeds of separation first took root—and gives us the opportunity to nurture ourselves into wholeness, into connection. Then we can plant fresh seeds of love, creating fertile ground for Unity and peace to flourish within and around us.

Each time we encounter recurring patterns in our lives we learn to journey back to the Origin seed to glean greater understanding. These patterns can appear in our relationships, moments of scarcity, or feelings of disconnection. By attuning to the Origin of shadow early sources of separation are illuminated. These sources stem from family lineage and past lives, but most often emerge from our childhood experiences.

We can reclaim our innocence—our pure and untouchable essence—by reconnecting with the awe and wonder that has always been part of us. The spark of imagination and creativity many of us felt as children is still alive within us, waiting to be rekindled. No matter what we have experienced or endured, we are not broken. The shadow, though it may feel powerful and even all consuming at times, does not possess control over us. While the shadow is part of us, it is not us. Imagine walking down the sidewalk as your shadow trails along, only existing as a byproduct of the Self. Physical and psychological shadows can only exist in certain circumstances—the angle of the sun must be just right to cast the shadow, just as only some experiences and relationships awaken our psycho-spiritual shadow.

What if remembering our true nature became a daily practice? Could nurturing our inner child become a regular and sacred ritual in our lives? By dedicating time each day to sit with compassion and reconnect with the younger versions of ourselves, we begin to mend the fractures between our past and present—creating Unity within us.

Through this introspective practice, we see the Origin seeds of separation that took root in our hearts, minds, and lives. The beliefs we naïvely adopted as children come to light and the shadow begins to fade. We begin to see Unity and truth beyond the false whispers of separation that "we are not safe, worthy, or loveable." These seeds, although hidden deep in the soil of our subconscious, gave rise to subtle patterns that in turn shaped our reality and experiences. Even as children, some part of us—our wise Divine witness—knew these beliefs were illusions, yet they often still became entrenched and reified by our culture of separation. While this part of us may have always known the deep truth, without the words to express it we often felt unseen, unheard, or gravely misunderstood—thereby creating the wounded inner child and subsequent shadow.

As we embark on this inner work as adults we are blessed with the tools to heal and transform into Unity. Each time we engage with this process of reliving and rewriting our story, we unravel the buried tangled knots that keep us stuck and nurture our innate wholeness. As we remind ourselves that we are worthy of love—not because of what we do, but simply because we are alive—we shed the shackles of conditional love and step into the infinity of Unity. Through these daily acts of remembrance, we draw closer to our true nature, allowing greater authenticity, freedom, and joy to emerge in our lives.

When feelings of being unheard or diminished arise, try to remember the Origin seed of that experience from your childhood and then envelop your inner child with boundless love. While challenging, also embrace the feeling of sadness and powerlessness that formed the shadow, offering your ultimate compassion to these painful parts. It is from this tender space that you can resolve separation patterns and sprout new Unity beliefs that nourish your true Divine nature.

161

You are not small...

You are infinitely loved...

You possess great power...

By maintaining a consistent vibrational frequency aligned with Unity, we develop greater confidence in transforming illusions when they surface. This requires trusting our natural state of love, despite thoughts that may challenge our purpose or spiritual sovereignty. Each moment is an opportunity for growth.

With our next breath, we courageously embrace the unknown, acknowledging our wholeness, creating room for the shadow self to be seen. Imagine wholeheartedly leaping into the boundless vibration of love, leaving behind all past feelings of shame and guilt. This transformative journey can evoke tears of relief. Although it can be both daunting and fulfilling, it is a pivotal step toward embodying Unity. Given the cathartic nature, it may even feel exhilarating.

We are all connected. The suffering in the world is a reflection of the suffering within. How we engage with others mirrors how we relate to ourselves. Is judgment or compassion our guiding light?

Confronting the uncomfortable aspects of ourselves and the collective can be challenging, especially when this clear sight reveals the injustices, inequalities, systemic issues, and lens of separation clouding our reality.

Allowing ourselves to fully experience emotions is a part of the healing and evolutionary process. It signifies our willingness to confront and acknowledge the truth. While this may feel overwhelming at times, it is important we remember that all emotions arise for a reason and are reflections, manifestations, and embodiments of our empathetic and compassionate hearts that desire Unity. When *emotions* are

162

allowed to be in motion versus being suppressed into stagnation, they are powerful alchemical forces that can be channeled into constructive action—sparking positive change for the individual and collective.

Have a good cry for humanity, for the animals, and for ourselves. While we no longer wish to embody the shame and guilt that has permeated our existence for many years, we may need to feel the weight of these beliefs to release them. We may feel angry and sad at the same time. All is welcome in Unity, it is part of the process. There is no wrong or right way to feel. Remember, just as every being has a Divine Unity purpose, so does every emotion—it is simply a matter of how we feel, integrate, and alchemize what arises.

When the shadow is given space to reveal the reasons for its existence, it becomes an enlightened teacher on our path. Learning to express our shadow in healthy ways is an adventure of exploration and may even feel joyful due to the healing it inspires. This process provides an opportunity to integrate the darker and hidden aspects of ourselves—this is the embodiment of Unity. Expressing shadow energy through art—be it music, literature, dance, or the visual arts—is a potent way to delve into the depths of human experience and bring some of the gems to the surface. Consensual and healthy expressions of sexuality can also serve as a powerful means for individuals to explore and integrate shadow aspects of themselves and bring them into their relationship.

Practices to Transform Shadow Energy

Patience: Healing and integrating shadow energy requires time and effort. Embrace patience as you navigate this journey of self-discovery and growth. ."everything in nature is accomplished and never rushes"

Cultivate gentleness: When negative thoughts arise from your inner critic, do your best to observe them in the neutrality of Love.

Embrace compassion: Recognize that shadow energy is a manifestation of the separation paradigm, it is NOT you. Remember the shadow has served as protection, bringing you to this moment.

Foster self-love: Embrace and accept yourself fully, including all shadow aspects. Love and validate yourself unconditionally. Acknowledge that your shadow and the elemental patterns are gradually being resolved. This is Unity in action.

Express gratitude and appreciation: Make it a concerted habit to offer gratitude and appreciation for this meandering journey of Self exploration and evolution as often as you can.

Creative expression: Give your shadow a creative outlet. Demystify the shadow through giving it voice, allow it to be seen. The act of expression will help dispel it.

The journey of transforming the shadow is akin to peeling back the layers of an onion. Each layer reveals another separation pattern that is ready to be seen and healed. The magnetic pull of the shadow cannot be denied. It is natural at times to feel drawn to its depths and various manifestations.

Even while on the path of evolution, we may occasionally indulge in behaviors rooted in the shadow. We might feel a desire to break the rules that have kept us feeling caged. There are no rigid rules when it comes to releasing and healing the shadow within.

As we embark on the path of Unity and personal empowerment, we may encounter resistance from people that are accustomed to our old ways of being. Shedding our former ways and embracing our authentic Self can create ripples of discomfort—growing pains—in ourselves and in our environment. People in our community, who are consumed by their shadow, may attempt to lure us back into the familiar territory of our previous Self. This resistance to change stems from the human tendency to gravitate toward the known, even if it means sacrificing our growth and evolution—ironically, our very purpose for existing!

As we embody Unity, we possess a higher vibration making those around us feel fearful of us without knowing exactly why. Their shadow may sense a threat being around us due to the powers of transmission, for simply being in the presence of an awakened Unity vibration may initiate the resolution of shadow patterns.

Assuming responsibility for all parts of ourselves involves recognizing when the shadow is reacting, so we are less likely to succumb to it and through our awareness are able to transmute the shadow into healing energy. Allow the shadow to emerge, see it clearly, and then allow it to fall away by responding gratefully from the heart.

Herbal Insights: St. John's Wort, Lavender, Chamomile & Willow

☽ **Best Ways to Connect:** Tea | Tincture | Infused Oil | Ritual Bathing

🌿 **St. John's Wort** *(Hypericum perforatum)* – **Light in the Darkness**
St. John's Wort is a herb of emotional resilience, warmth, and nervous system healing. She has long been used to lift heavy emotions, ease stagnation, and restore balance. When grief feels overwhelming, St. John's Wort serves as a gentle light, reminding us that healing comes in cycles. She is especially supportive for those who feel stuck in sadness or weighed down by emotional burdens.

☽ **Ways to Connect:** Drink as a tea for emotional support | Use infused oil for nervous system balance | Work with the plant spirit in meditation for renewal

🌿 **Lavender** *(Lavandula angustifolia)* – **Calm & Emotional Restoration** Lavender is a beloved ally for soothing the heart, mind, and body. She offers comfort during grief, easing anxiety and promoting relaxation. When sorrow causes restlessness or an unsettled heart, lavender provides a sense of deep peace and emotional grounding.

☽ **Ways to Connect:** Diffuse lavender essential oil for relaxation | Drink as a tea before bed | Add to a bath for nervous system support

🌿 **Chamomile** *(Matricaria chamomilla)* – **Gentle Healing & Soft Release**
Chamomile is a tender and nurturing plant that soothes raw emotions and eases tension in the nervous system. She is especially supportive for those experiencing emotional exhaustion or numbness, bringing emotions into balance

166

without overwhelm. Chamomile gently invites release, offering comfort to both body and spirit.

☽ **Ways to Connect:** Brew into a tea for relaxation | Carry dried chamomile as a comforting talisman | Use chamomile-infused oil in gentle self-massage

🌿 **Willow** *(Salix spp.)* – **Surrender & Transformation**
Willow teaches the art of surrender and emotional flow. Just as she bends with the wind rather than breaking, Willow guides us through grief with grace, allowing emotions to move freely without resistance. Often associated with mourning and resilience, she helps us process sorrow without becoming lost in it.

☽ **Ways to Connect:** Sit with a willow tree for grounding | Use willow flower essence for emotional release | Add willow bark to ritual baths to encourage surrender and deep healing

These four plant allies work beautifully together, offering comfort, resilience, and gentle support through grief and transformation. 🌿

The shadow is nothing more than whispers of the soul,
Calling for the sun to burn away the veil,
Revealing the golden threads of remembrance,
Where dark and light become one.

CHAPTER TWELVE

EMBODIEMENT

THE EARTH IS OUR BODY & OUR BODY IS THE EARTH

We are one with the body. The body is not separate from Earth. Earth is not separate from the Universe. We are one Love, one organism, working together in the energetic field of potentiality.

The human body is a living, breathing miracle. Animalistic in nature, our body is both an earthly vessel and a celestial creation offering unique gifts to Life. It is time to embody our Divine purpose.

The body is often perceived as separate from our inner knowing and energetic field. We are rarely encouraged to listen to the body, despite the body constantly listening and responding to us. Every thought, word, and belief we project influences our body's vibration and vitality. We have been taught to view the body as merely a mechanical vessel, detached from the unifying vessel of love.

The body is much more than a physical structure; it is a dynamic quantum system in constant communication with the vast energy fields interconnecting all things. This profound reality often escapes our awareness because we live under the illusion of separation. We call it the illusion of separation precisely because it exists in the realm of the unconscious—hidden beneath layers of conditioning and unawareness. This illusion is not the truth of our true nature; it is a veil preventing us from fully perceiving the Unity binding all life together. The Earth and the Universal Mind are One. Embodiment far surpasses soma, "of the body." Embodiment is Living our true nature into existence by attuning to and integrating the infinite information coursing through us at all times. The awakening process requires becoming aware of and attuned to the universal energies moving within and around us—allowing our physical, emotional, and spiritual selves to harmonize in coherence.

Embodiment is a deeply personal journey and complex process that involves opening the heart; restructuring belief systems; healing the nervous system; detoxifying the blood and organs; revitalizing neuroplasticity in the mind; reconnecting heart and mind; creating coherence to feed Unity. Each facet works together to raise our bodily vibration and in turn activates dormant DNA.

Every species—human, animal, or plant—contains a collective energetic body rooted in a unique Origin seed. This energetic seed provides the blueprint for that species purpose, shaping its collective experience. The human collective energetic body is particularly intricate, much like mycelium networks that connect mushroom colonies and enable the transfer of nutrients and chemical signals. Science shows how mushrooms thrive within these networks, creating symbiotic relationships that support entire ecosystems. Similarly, the collective human body acts as one interconnected organism, sharing evolutionary wisdom and resonating with a unified vibrational field that intertwines each human, much like the fungi shaping the soil beneath our feet.

Due to human's dynamic interconnection, when an individual embodies Unity it affects the whole, thereby elevating the collective human frequency bit by bit. Like mycelium, there is no separation. When one part of the network is strengthened, it supports the whole—when one human aligns with Unity, it ripples out, influencing the greater human body.

By casting our gaze inward and furthering our personal embodiment, we participate in the collective's vibrational shift. Each individual's evolution furthers the cultivation of a harmonious and unified global consciousness. As individuals increasingly align with the Unity within, the collective human body moves toward embodying Unity at an exquisite and exponential rate.

Within this enhanced rate of evolution, there are no shortcuts or spiritual bypasses. The process of clearing stagnant energy and elemental patterns takes time. Embodiment is a steady process requiring great patience and consistent practice. However, as the vibration of the collective body rises from personal shifts, it will become easier and faster for individuals beginning their journey of alignment and awakening. Like raindrops rolling down glass—when one merges into another, together they gain unstoppable momentum and pave the way for others to follow.

While embodiment may seem like an individual journey, it is through relationships and service to the community that the process accelerates. Connecting with others who are attuned to both personal and collective evolution can ease feelings of isolation while encouraging mutual learning and support. As more people awaken, our community naturally expands. Being in service to Life—whether to fellow humans or other living beings—is one of the most powerful ways to cultivate community and, in turn, deepen our embodiment. By its very nature, Unity cannot be embodied in isolation; it must be shared, woven, and created through connection.

From these places of service, a new purpose will emerge. While the purpose that arises is individual, at its core, it remains in service to the human collective body and the entirety of nature.

Embodiment is the actionable state of living in Unity, an ever-expanding intelligence. Unlike beliefs instilled by external systems, Unity beliefs arise from within us as we align with and embody the Unity paradigm.

Beyond integrating and embodying Unity values into our thoughts, words, and actions, we may experience heightened senses of somatic awareness and greater presence in this physical body. Attuning to and aligning with our inner landscape is one way Unity can be experienced within us. As we deepen our embodiment our physical sense gates become to heighten, thereby bolstering our connection with Life beyond our skin. Smells, sounds, sights, and touch become more vivid and alive. This increased awareness can elevate our emotional experience of each moment, reminding us of Life's intimate interconnection.

Through embodiment, we reclaim the freedom
to unlock and fully embrace the authentic free will
That has always been our birthright.

As neuroplasticity in the mind expands, thoughts and ideas flow more effortlessly from the Universal Mind. In turn, we are more likely to experience creative flow states unimpeded by the lens of illusion, whether it manifests as shadow or another form of separation. This fluidity of information is vital to embodying the Unity paradigm, requiring that our channels remain clear. The newly cultivated trust in inner knowing and the ability to take action from these flow states is where embodiment begins to transform the external reality we create.

Living embodiment resembles being nurtured within a mother's womb where our needs are ever met with love and we are held in water's warmest embrace. Through the Divinity of water, we co-create with the universe. Water serves as the bridge between the energetic biofield and the physical body, serving as a vehicle—a vessel—for information to flow. In its purest state, water reflects the neutrality of Love in physical form. Water is life! Water is Unity!

The emerging Unity paradigm has already reset the water in a future timeline. As previously mentioned, from that origin seed, there is a gradual resetting of all waters, mirroring and supporting our individual cellular processes. Water serves as a catalyst for trusting our inner knowing, with its fluidity as its superpower. Not only does water carry information to and from our inner knowing, integrating wisdom throughout the entire system, but it also clears stagnation, reducing entropy and increasing our capacity to receive information. All of this creates vibrational continuity that activates dormant celestial DNA embedded within the body.

As we resolve repetitive, habitual thought patterns rooted in beliefs of separation that once drained our energy, we open ourselves to a greater capacity to trust our inner knowing. Cultivating this trust is linked embodiment as this "knowing" stems from deep within us—our well of wisdom, our gut sense. As we practice listening to our intuition we are simultaneously learning to hear and honor our body's knowing versus the all mighty mind. It is here that our mind, body, and spirit merge into Unity, meeting in the neutrality of Love.

Embodiment exists deep within the cellular level of our Being. While it may seem that the mind leads the way in making decisions to further our evolution and embodiment, true growth is sustained at our cellular core. That said, the mind is certainly part of the process—an integral component—but, to our dismay, it is not the leader. Without the body, neither mind nor spirit could exist, for the body is our vessel, the fertile soil from which all else grows. The truth is, without cultivated heart-mind coherence, the mind is nothing more than a memory bank, relying solely on external input.

As a Unity vibration is rooted in the body—within each cell—Unity leaves the conceptual realm and is made manifest, a lived experience woven into our every action.

174

Water is life,
She is the all knowing heart of God.
Her compassionate love is at the heart of embodiment.

Everything we experience—every challenge, every gift—offers us an opportunity for growth. Each step guides us toward greater embodiment. It is not a question of *if* we will embody Unity, but rather a matter of *when*. Whether we are consciously aware of it or not, the process is unfolding within each of us.

It is okay if it feels confusing, foreign, or overwhelming to conceptualize this information. We do not need to fully grasp or even track every aspect of our awakening! The intent of sharing this information is merely to support the process—offering guide posts to ease the worrying mind and to spark inspiration. Rest assured, we are ALL on the path to embodying Unity.

There are many practices we can explore to help our bodies align with and embody Unity. When embraced, these practices support us in allowing the fullness of Unity to emerge from within. Practices range from increasing somatic mindfulness; to grounding; to enlivening and awakening our energy and vitality; to dissolving boundaries of separation, rejecting the notion of an isolated self and embracing interconnectedness; to trusting our innate intuition and inner knowing over the doubting, rational mind.

As we reflect, we might ask ourselves: How often do you truly listen to your body? Can you recognize the subtle signals the body sends? Do you respond with caring intention and love? Our bodies are always speaking to us and seeking connection, balance, and alignment. Are we listening?

Somatic Meditation
Full-Body Connection and Dialogue

This somatic meditation guides you through a journey of connecting deeply with your body, engaging in conversation with your cellular structures, lymphatic system, bones, arteries, and water molecules. By fostering this dialogue, you activate your body's innate wisdom and create harmony throughout your entire being.

Begin by finding a quiet, comfortable space. Close your eyes and take slow, deep breaths, letting your body relax. Shift your awareness to your toes, feeling their connection to the earth. Imagine energy flowing into your feet, awakening the lymphatic vessels, bones, and cells. Inquire, "What do I need to feel balanced and supported in this moment?" Pause to sense any subtle sensations, emotions, or insights in response.

As your awareness moves up your legs, feel the strength of your calves, thighs, and hips. Visualize blood flowing freely through your arteries and lymphatic fluids clearing stagnation. Picture the water molecules in these areas vibrating with vitality. Ask these parts of your body, "How can I support your strength and flow?" Listen for a response, it may come as a feeling, thought, or physical shift.

Bring your attention to your lower abdomen, sense the rhythm of your lymphatic organs—such as the spleen and lymph nodes in your hip flexor region, under your arms, and by your thyroid—working in harmony with your digestive system. Visualize water molecules in your cells integrating wisdom and vitality. Breathe deeply and ask, "What wisdom do you hold for me today?" Allow the sensations or insights to emerge naturally.

Shift your focus to your chest and heart. Feel the gentle rhythm of your heartbeat as arteries carry life-giving blood and lymphatic vessels clear your system. Engage in dialogue with your heart, "What do you need to stay open and strong?" Picture water molecules amplifying your connection to love, resilience, and flow.

Finally, bring awareness to your neck, head, and entire body. Imagine energy coursing through your arteries and lymph nodes, clearing and nourishing your brain. Sense the water molecules vibrating with clarity and alignment. Ask your cells and water molecules, "What clarity can you offer me?" Expand your awareness to feel your body as a unified system and gently ask, "How can I honor and support our Unity?"

Conclude the meditation by taking a few grounding breaths, offering gratitude for your body and the wisdom it carries. Gently open your eyes and maintain this embodied conversation and connection into the rest of your day—allowing the insights to guide your actions and nurture your sense of wholeness.

When we listen deeply and honor what we hear, we can sense our body's natural desire to connect with the Earth. Earthing is a simple yet profoundly effective way to enhance the flow of energy within us as well as find solid ground to rest upon. Standing barefoot on the ground, or wearing grounding footwear, allows Earth's energy to stabilize and recharge our system. Just as a loose ground wire can drain a car battery, neglecting to ground ourselves can result in scattered energy, leaving us feeling depleted. Earthing recharges our electromagnetic biofields, aligning us with the rising paradigm of Unity.

As we enter a time of more frequent and larger solar flares reaching Earth—a potent and essential component of the awakening process—the need for grounding becomes even more essential. Solar flares carry intense bursts of energy from the sun and, interestingly, can feel both disorienting and uplifting.

From a metaphysical perspective, solar flares act as catalysts for spiritual awakening, highlighting areas of stagnation and initiating the release of outdated beliefs rooted in separation. Grounding during these energetic shifts helps stabilize the biofield, supporting the body as it resolves lingering elemental patterns while sparking newly formed patterns in Unity. These shifts create a sustained higher resonant frequency within the body. As this vibration continues to rise, dormant cellular codes activate, further accelerating the embodiment process.

These flares enhance what is already unfolding, offering a powerful surge of energy. Once activated, these refined cellular structures support a deeper embodiment of Unity, allowing for a quantum inner knowing to manifest.

We can breathe ourselves into embodiment. As previously discussed, each breath completes an elemental cycle—where expansion and contraction reflect the balancing of masculine and feminine energies in the body. This rhythmic exchange creates an alchemical fusion that binds us in Unity, while simultaneously sustaining the body's life force.

When we become aware of each breath, the parasympathetic nervous system nourishes the system—reducing stress and calming the mind and body as we exit fight-flight-freeze responses. Breathing is far more than regulating oxygen and carbon dioxide levels; it is a primary energy exchange, fueling our vitality and every subsequent bodily process as well as all emotional and psycho-spiritual endeavors. Conscious breathing also enhances cellular function, improving the flow of energy and oxygenation throughout the system, which in turn raises the body's vibrational frequency. Breath is Life's greatest sustainer!

When we practice conscious breathing, we recondition the body into optimal breath—enhancing oxygen transportation and supporting cellular metabolism. Most of us have forgotten how to breathe deeply and naturally. By learning to balance both feminine and masculine energies through each breath, while making space for the neutrality of love, we foster Unity and support the journey to embodiment.

Element Practice:

Go to a stream, ocean, or any other body of Water. Touch your feet to the ground, either sitting in a chair or on the Earth. Breathe in the elements of Water, Fire, Wind, and Earth in one Unifying breath. You can also breathe in one element at a time. However you practice, the intention is the same—to connect the elements through your breath. Once you have the breath pattern established, imagine masculine energy descending into the crown chakra through the top of your head and feminine energy ascending through the root chakra, up through the perineum from the Earth—creating a spark of Love in the heart. While this can be practiced anywhere, it is particularly powerful when done outdoors.

For those of us who struggle with eating healthy foods, meditating, and staying physically active, it can be comforting to know that as we begin to embody a Unity vibration, we will naturally gravitate toward taking better care of our bodies. The struggle diminishes, and we find ourselves naturally drawn to eating whole, organic foods, moving our bodies, and meditating in our own way. The joy of being connected with our bodies becomes second nature as we embrace a new, seemingly effortless approach to self-care. The detox begins.

Altering the body's vibration does not result in an instantly "fit" body. Physical fitness does not equate to embodying Unity beliefs. You might be an accomplished runner, bodybuilder, or yogi and still hold separation beliefs that foster scarcity and fear within the body. On the other hand, someone who is overweight and cannot run a city block might have fully embodied Unity beliefs. Unity goes far beyond physical form and appearance.

While having a fit body is certainly desirable, it is important to recognize that we all reach embodiment in different ways. Movement is a key part of the embodiment process, but it is not the only factor. The journey to embodiment can also bring an increase in body weight and highlight dis-ease and chronic imbalances calling out for resolution. It is essential we let go of judgment when it comes to body appearance, for it is rooted in shallow separation beliefs.

So, let's get moving! Dance, groove, and sway with the rhythm of life. Engage in activities that resonate with your being, whether it is going for a walk, stretching, running, hiking, cycling, dancing, practicing yoga, or exploring qigong. The specific method does not matter. What matters most is that we move and embrace the joyous flow of the natural world. By doing so, we can embody a vibrant and harmonious way of living.

If we are in pain and moving feels difficult, explore other ways to move energy—be it very gentle, subtle seated qigong or singing. And if we find ourselves exercising without a conscious connection to the body, slow down and evoke a dialogue with the bodymind. Possibly try moving meditations—such as tai chi, qigong or intuitive dance—and allow your heart to guide the movement, releasing the "accomplishing" mind.

The type of breathing, movement, foods, and herbs that support increased embodiment are unique to each individual. Similarly, the amount of sleep, alone time, rest, dance, touch, and sex required varies for each person. While we can explore and embrace proven techniques that support these areas, self-empowerment and deep listening are the foundation for all forms of Embodiment. It is through this introspective practice that we can access the abundant flow of information from within.

Herbal Insights: Cilantro, Activated Charcoal, Turmeric & Neem

☽ **Best Ways to Use:** Fresh, tea, tincture, or powdered form.

🌿 **Cilantro** *(Coriandrum sativum)* – Deep Cellular Detoxification
Cilantro is a refreshing ally for clearing stagnation and supporting deep detoxification. It is known for its ability to bind to heavy metals and toxins, helping to guide them out of

the body. This vibrant herb also aids digestion and promotes a sense of lightness, both physically and energetically.

☽ **Ways to Connect:** Enjoy fresh in meals, blend into green juices, or take as a tincture to support daily cleansing.

🌿 **Activated Charcoal** – Absorption & Clearing Pathways
Activated charcoal carries a unique ability to absorb impurities and toxins, making space for greater vitality. It works by binding to unwanted substances and removing them from the body, clearing internal pathways and restoring energetic alignment.

☽ **Ways to Connect:** Mix with water and drink on an empty stomach, use in face masks for purification, or take as a capsule during deep cleansing.

🌿 **Turmeric** *(Curcuma longa)* & **Neem** *(Azadirachta indica)* – Synergistic Purification & Balance
Turmeric and neem work together to bring balance, supporting the immune system, circulation, and overall well-being. Turmeric's golden compounds nourish the body, reducing inflammation and enhancing cellular repair, while neem deeply cleanses and aids digestion, acting as a powerful bitter herb for detoxification.

☽ **Ways to Connect:** Take as a tea or tincture in the morning, blend with warm water, or incorporate into meals for sustained benefits.

Together, these powerful herbs create a foundation for purification, helping the body shed stagnation, release toxins, and align with a more vibrant state. 🌿 ☽ ✦

CHAPTER THIRTEEN

JOY!

AHHHH JOY!

Joy is a universal experience shared by all beings on Earth. It is at the core of appreciation and without it, life would be dull and uninspiring. Joy is a carefully crafted emotion, present in everything from plants to animals, and of course, in us humans. It shines through in moments of playfulness and delights in the Celebrating life is inherently joyful and makes every moment feel worthwhile.

Joy is not a product of the mind; it is entirely a matter of the heart. Simply uttering the word "Joy" can fill us with instant happiness.

So, what brings joy into your life?

While the journey of ascension can feel serious at times, awakening allows us to return to our hearts and rediscover the youthful exuberance of Joy. Unity can be playful, fun, and infused with Joy! Life should be abundant and enjoyable—no one should feel like they are on a never ending treadmill.

We are infinitely and incredibly blessed to live on the most beautiful planet—thank you Earth. Let us not lose sight of the immense joy awaiting us as we stoke Unity, reconnect with our true nature, and embody our connection to each other.

The Joy that arises from within us when we reconnect with nature and each other serves as a catalyst for our collective, unified purpose—a purpose that will initiate the revitalization of our ecosystem. Together in Unity, we will experience a profound Love that binds us all, both to each other and to Unity beliefs. As we remember the power of coming together in Unity, we will feel an ecstatic Joy so overwhelming that we will never want to turn back. Even as we face the challenges of ascension, Joy can be found in the profound changes we experience. Make it a priority to let go and have fun along the journey by embracing the beautiful mystery of surrendering to the moment.

Nature brings us Joy in so many ways, from the gentle warmth of the sun on our backs to the symphony of birdsong in the morning. Embodying Joy is a natural state of being—a blissful dance through the beauty of life—just like a hummingbird joyfully dancing from one flower to another.

Let's prioritize activities that bring us Joy. Ignite your creative spark and truly let yourself live a little...or a lot! We need free time to savor life, and this is the essence of Unity. It is important to recognize that the reality we are moving toward is spacious and Joyful. The vibration of Unity allows each of us to choose our paths based on inspiration and enthusiasm. We will have the space to express our individuality while simultaneously creating in harmony with nature. This is the full embodiment of Joy!

The days of enduring jobs we dread are soon coming to an end. If that sounds too good to be true, it's time to let go of that belief. Life doesn't have to be so hard! That being said, everything we are going through is guiding us towards a more Joyful, Unity existence.

We got this!

Even in the face of adversity, Joy can still be found. It reminds us that life is full of ups and downs and that we have the power to choose how we respond. When we embrace Joy, we open ourselves to new possibilities and experiences that we may have never fully imagined before.

Intolerance and negativity have no place in a Joy-filled world. As we awaken to the interconnectedness of all life, we realize that we are all in this together, supporting and nourishing each other. By spreading Love and kindness, we create a ripple that transforms the world around us.

Let us embrace joy's tender touch and allow it to be our guide on this wondrous journey of life. With open hearts and minds, we have the power to weave a world of endless possibilities and boundless abundance.

So, let us dance!
      Let us laugh!
            Let us sing!
                  Let joy be our constant companion!

Herbal Insights: Violet, Lilac & Daisy

☽ **Best Ways to Use:** Tea, tincture, infused oil, floral baths, or as fresh flowers in sacred spaces.

🌿 **Violet** *(Viola odorata)* – **Heart Healing & Gentle Joy**
Violet carries a soft, nurturing energy that gently dissolves sadness, grief, and emotional stagnation. It creates space for peace, self-love, and quiet joy, reminding us that happiness can be subtle, soothing, and deeply nourishing.

☽ **Ways to Connect:** Brew as tea for emotional support, blend fresh violets with spring water to drink, or infuse in oil for heart-centered self-care.

🌿 **Lilac** *(Syringa spp.)* – **Uplifting Renewal & Lightheartedness**
Lilac embodies the essence of spring, clearing emotional heaviness and inviting fresh joy and optimism. Its uplifting fragrance washes away stagnant energy, bringing a sense of lightness and playfulness.

☽ **Ways to Connect:** Place fresh lilacs in your space for an instant mood lift, add to a bath for emotional cleansing, or sit near a lilac tree to welcome new beginnings.

🌿 **Daisy** *(Bellis perennis)* – **Innocence & Simple Happiness**
Daisy carries a bright, uncomplicated energy that inspires wonder, resilience, and joy. It helps ease overthinking and emotional burdens, guiding us to embrace the present with curiosity and an open heart.

☽ **Ways to Connect:** Drink as tea for emotional upliftment, weave fresh daisies into flower crowns for lighthearted energy, or place in your space to encourage joy and playfulness.

Together, Violet, Lilac, and Daisy create a beautiful balance of deep healing, renewal, and childlike joy—supporting the heart with grace, ease, and an open spirit. 🌿 ☾ ✦

CHAPTER FOURTEEN

❧

SEXUALITY

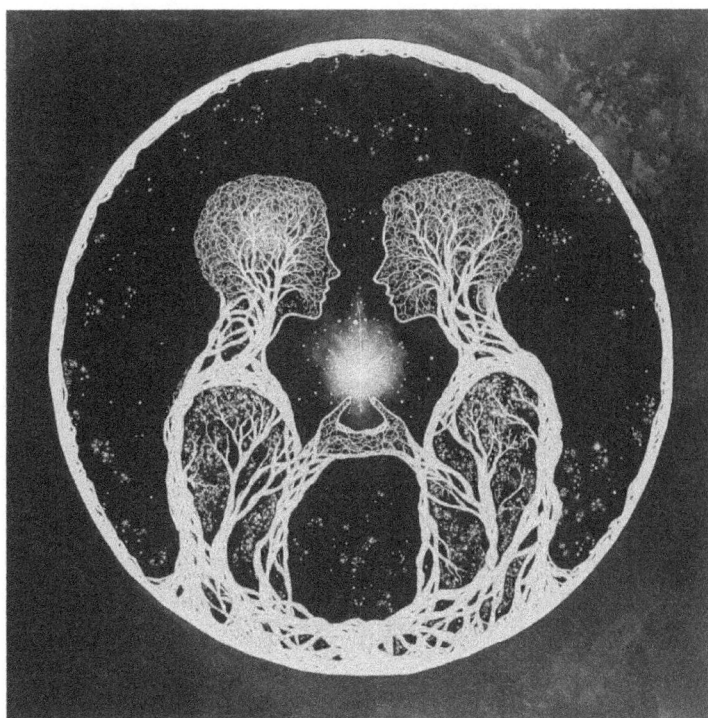

SEXUAL & SPIRITUAL SOVEREIGNTY
ARE ESSENTIAL KEYS TO AWAKENING. THEY ARE
INTERMITTENLY INTERWOVEN AND DIRECTLY,
INFORM ONE ANOTHER.

Sexuality is a Joyful expression of embodiment. Sexual energy, regardless of gender or sexual orientation, represents the merging of feminine and masculine energies. When these energies unite between two people, they create a euphoric spark, forming a connection that sends ripples of Unity out from the heart in all directions. This is the healing essence of a Divine Union—a safe container to see and be seen, feel fully, offer new life to our wounded part, and share in the most fulfilling experience of oneness with another human.

The energy of sexuality is often overlooked as a path to awakening. Engaging intentionally with this energy offers a connection with the Divine during moments of blissful surrender. Here, in the name of Joy, we can heal generational patterns created by violence and the shaming of sexuality that inhibit our individual growth and the evolution of our ancestral lineage. Soul connections with another person are rare; therefore, when they do happen take note.

The ultimate beauty of Divine Unions lay in the deeper emotional layers that transcend physicality. There is an inner knowing, something sacred and unique to each Divine Union. It is as if the two people complete each other in a mystical way.

Divine Unions are both deeply challenging and profoundly exhilarating. When two people enter this sacred connection, the vibration within their bodies rises instantly. This energetic shift defines a Divine Union and begins dissolving entrenched beliefs around sexual separation. As we've explored, unraveling these patterns involves addressing the emotional imprints stored in the body. In this space of heightened connection, insecurities, stigmas, trust issues, and unresolved traumas naturally come to the surface, seeking recognition and the opportunity for healing.

If we are not prepared or have not yet developed the skills to communicate what we are feeling, as we begin resolving sexual separation beliefs we might feel the urge to run away or project these emotions onto our partner. It is essential we give ourselves and our partner time to process arising emotions with the utmost Love and offer patience as we unpack vulnerable experiences, for it can be challenging and incredibly tender. Love and patience cannot eliminate tenderness, but can support us as we ride the waves. We may need to step back for a while from both ourselves or our partner, offering space for the unfolding. This emotional processing inevitably leads to authentic communication with our partner, furthering our respective and shared evolution. The almighty Love will hold the Divine Union together as long as we continue to see clearly and not allow triggers to tear us apart.

Divine Unions that can navigate these vibrational upgrades without separating can greatly accelerate the embodiment process. We will begin to see more Divine Unions emerge, resulting in powerful, enlightened couples ready to serve each other and the collective wholeheartedly.

We currently live in a hyper-sexualized culture rooted in oppression. This has led to a diminished understanding of sexuality's purpose beyond physical pleasure and procreation. From this cultural blindspot, many relationships experience sexual stagnation and thus fail to grow together. Fading sexual fulfillment has become normalized and even anticipated. Many relationships however, are dormant Divine Unions waiting to reinvent themselves—like a butterfly emerging from a cocoon. That said, other relationships may dissolve, for the difference in vibration is too great.

A Divine Union is guided and sustained by deep trust and feeling of being held in a safe container within the Union. This trust forms a strong foundation to explore the parts of ourselves that long to be seen. As partners resolve patterns together through authentic curiosity, raw vulnerability, compassion, and passion, intimacy grows within the partnership.

This leads to fulfilling and passionate sexual experiences, illuminating the connection between the emotional, spiritual, and physical body. The merging of the feminine and masculine energies can be felt in profound new ways as the sense of oneness deepens, creating a whole-body experience of blissful and expansive sexual connection.

Pursuing or actively seeking a Divine Union can interfere with its natural unfolding. Instead, inviting it with intention and trusting it to manifest when the timing aligns allows for a more harmonious process. Like many things in life, Divine Unions require intention, faith, and patience to come to fruition. Such connections are unlikely to appear out of nowhere but often arise through stepping into the world and being present in spaces where meaningful opportunities can arise.

Everyone deserves such a Union. As we draw closer to Embodiment, the Divine Union plays an important part of shifting our inner landscapes. Most of us are not really sure what one is as a true divine union has the power to pull us into Unity. Although we may not have experienced such a Union before, we may imagine what it would be like to co-create one.

The great illusion is forgetting that we have been in a Divine Union with ourselves since the moment we were born. Nevertheless, it will take time to shed the protective husks that keep us from merging with those parts of ourselves that ultimately allow us to feel the constantness of our inner Union.

We are whole and divine and interconnected to sexuality This perceived internal separation extends to our sexual relationships, creating a sense of inherent disconnection.

When we think of sexual healing and Divine Union, our minds often envision two individuals coming together in a sacred connection. While this is a beautiful and valid expression of divine union, it is not the only one. Divine Union can also be a deeply personal journey—a transformative sexual relationship we cultivate within ourselves. Though often overlooked, this inner exploration holds profound potential for healing and growth.

As we embark on this journey inward, we may find ourselves transmuting old energies and separation beliefs that impede the flow of sexual energy. This flow guides us toward a greater awareness of our body and what truly excites and turns us on. This process often requires time alone with our body and space to reflect and reevaluate what sexuality means to us from this sacred perspective. Many of us may realize that we've rarely explored an honest, nurturing relationship with our own sexuality, and we might not fully understand our desires, boundaries, or what truly brings us pleasure.

In this sacred space of self-discovery, we have the opportunity to embrace our truths without the guilt or shame of self-touch, or the external pressure we may feel when with a lover. By releasing judgment and societal narratives around self-pleasure, we can begin to reclaim the pure potential of our sexual energy. Reaching orgasm in ways we have not previously experienced can be explored while alone, though, of course, it can also be done with a lover. Divine union represents the balanced state of the masculine and feminine energies—a spark of Unity manifested through the orgasm. This balance holds immense power for transformation, allowing us to shatter preconceived notions about the significance of these moments of release and pure ecstasy.

For those who have difficulty achieving orgasm, practicing alone can help create new pathways to reach this state. The orgasm can even be a tool to bring us closer to a Unity vibration. For men, this might mean exploring the prostate orgasm, which is closer to the deeper, earth-shattering experience a woman may have through her G-spot. Both emerge from the core of the sexual energy center, offering a profound connection to our inner essence. As a collective, we are just beginning to let go of the hollow shell of sexuality we were born into. From these places, we can open portals to a Unity paradigm.

By cultivating this deeper awareness and honoring the flows of our own sexuality while alone, we prepare ourselves for more authentic and fulfilling connections with our lovers. When we enter relationships from a place of Unity, we bring with us newly formed pathways, offering them as sacred gifts to share with our partners.

Sexuality carries vibrational keys to ascension. In a holistic and expansive way, incredible pleasure and moments of true presence can be experienced within sexual flows, In turn, this can lead to transcendental pathways that enhance our inner knowing. These energies are creation itself! The potency of this energy is why we feel such profound presence when we achieve orgasm. The nature of creation is blissful, ecstatic, and deeply connected with water and its life-giving abilities. For this reason, we can believe that sexuality is a conduit for conceiving a higher vibration through Joy and love in Unity.

Sensuality is like honey for the senses—sweet and nourishing. Its subtle nature is found everywhere, adding richness to life far beyond sexual interactions. Without it, life would be dull and colorless. From biting into a juicy peach; to the scent of blooming roses; to a slight breeze blowing between our clothes and skin; to the gentle caress of a lover, sensuality infuses life with connection. It is the healing balm that reminds us how precious life is and what a gift it is to be in a body on Earth. We are truly blessed in so many ways. Sensuality is a reminder to keep a grateful heart.

Sensuality can be embraced as a way of life, offering the sweet connective energy that binds us. Yet, within the paradigm of separation, this vital essence seems to have been diminished. In our modern world, we have grown rigid—out of necessity—becoming overly cautious in protecting ourselves from unwanted sexual advances. People may also hesitate to share moments of innocent sensuality with others, fearing misunderstanding or judgment. This fear-based hesitance has roots in a deeper truth... As a species, we have drifted far from the innocence that we once fully embodied. In losing this innocence, we also lost the sweet and tender expression of sensuality—a natural and loving way to explore and celebrate the beauty of connection through sexuality.

By anticipating sexual shadows to be present in every sexual relationship, be it lurking in the corner or center stage, we are not blindsided when they emerge. Sexuality, like everything else, mirrors the reality in which we live. So, if our wounds begin to overpower our clear sight it is an invitation to inquire within and offer these ouchy parts unconditional Love and attention. As previously discussed, when a sexual partnership is not actively triggering and held with great intention, these wounded parts can receive profound healing from being in relation.

Just as we can express light, we can also act out shadow; however, both can bring immense healing. Within the bounds of consent and deep Love, nothing is taboo. Simply talking about our desires and fantasies can release their hold over us.

And, if we choose to act them out within the boundaries of sexual adventure and play then they might even resolve the separation paradigm living in our sexual bodies. Within the realm of intimacy—whether it involves gentle, fierce, or animalistic passions—we find liberation and self-discovery. We venture beyond the confines of societal norms and expectations, embracing the richness and diversity of our desires. It is here, amidst the complexities of our yearnings and the raw intensity of the unknown, that we uncover hidden facets of ourselves. In this space, we revel in the beauty of our multiplicity, surrendering to the intoxicating interplay of vulnerability, intensity, and untethered pleasure. There is not "one" way to engage in sexual play or to experience the healing that often follows such play.

When we trust, we feel safe & when we feel safe, we trust. When we rest in safety, the vibration in our bodies increases. Our nervous system relaxes and internal thoughts slow, allowing our inner knowing to awaken. In a Divine Union, we can create a vibrational container close to a Unity vibration, leading us to uncharted territories of transcendence. In this exchange of desires
and Divinity, the boundaries between self and soul dissolve and we are immersed in a boundless ocean of ecstasy.

The healthiest relationships are the truthful ones, grounded in Presence not a fantasy or projection of what the relationship "should be," and shared commitment to living in truth. In a sacred container two souls can share their authentic, real-time, embodied selves with each other—revealing their deepest truths, their raw messy vulnerability, unresolved patterns, and even their most shameful thoughts. There may be ruptures, misunderstandings, intense feelings of doubt, anger, fear, anxiety and groundlessness along the way, but security lives in the mutual willingness to face whatever arises. This requires us to be vulnerable—to say "My heart hurts. I am in pain. I feel deep sorrow," while not unduly blaming our

196

partner. We learn we have to express, "I need support right now" to receive it. We listen and hear one another, honoring each other's wounds without judgment. In these bonds we learn to share our desires, hopes, longings, and dreams and not expect or command the other person to see things the same way. We release the expectation that this ONE person could meet your every need. We receive their "noes" and "yeses," even if it hurts at first. Together, we stand in the moment both unwavering and uncertain as the winds of change blow around us.

We stand together in the heat of transformation—in the unknown—trusting our connection to be stronger from the storm. We learn to open ourselves wholeheartedly to the fear of rejection, trusting we will still be loved in our naked truth. We practice holding one another in moments of uncertainty—embodying Unity as the perfect mess that we are. From this place, we inspire and heal each other, forming a lasting bond that fosters sexual oneness and creates the infinite spark of Love. This is the Divine Union .

The Unity paradigm's crystalline structure originates from a Divine Union, a sacred convergence of energies that gave birth to its foundational seed. This paradigm was born through the profound Love shared between ascended masters, where the spark of their intimate encounters ignited a new field of consciousness. From this union, the essence of Unity emerged, forming a blueprint that we are now beginning to embody.

As this concept may feel controversiaL take what resonates and leave the rest. The invitation here is to reflect on why and how this perspective challenges our core beliefs and what within us feels unsettled by its implications.

Unity consciousness—also known as Christ consciousness—was originally ignited through the sacred union of Jesus Christ and Mary Magdalene. In the profound energy of their shared orgasm, a portal of light was opened, birthing the Unity paradigm into existence. This often-overlooked or deliberately ignored truth serves as a reminder that true Unity requires both the feminine and masculine to be fully present in physical form. Without this balance, the embodiment of Unity remains incomplete.

Is it blasphemy to consider the possibility of an ascended master engaging sexually within a Divine Union? Or, does this notion merely confront deeply ingrained perceptions and ideologies of spirituality and enlightenment and therefore feels uncomfortable?

Why do so many religious texts elevate the masculine as the sole bearer of enlightenment while portraying the feminine as pure, untouchable, and virginal? This perspective diminishes the power of the feminine and offers an incomplete understanding of spiritual wholeness—of Unity. Around the same time that Unity consciousness was born the illusion of separation emerged—a divide that unjustly suppresses the transformative power of sexuality.

The brutal killing of Jesus Christ and the stoning of Mary Magdalene sent a clear and tragic message: to embody a Divine Union was dangerous and a threat to societal structures of the era. This suppression of sacred sexuality and Divine Union reinforced fear and shame, discouraging the embodiment of such connections. Yet beneath these layers of fear lies the unshaken truth that Unity is created through the harmonious synergy of feminine and masculine energies—thereby rejecting all notions of hierarchy, honoring both as essential and Divine.

Rituals imbued with sacred sexuality were once honored and practiced by humankind, recognizing the great powers imbedded in awakening sexual energy. These practices however have been intentionally erased from historical records, directly influencing what society deems to be acceptable and "true." Since the powers of Unity within us have been latent—not yet ready to be unveiled—humans have had to wait for over two thousand years for the Unity paradigm to emerge on the collective level. However, individuals and Divine Unions across cultures have contributed to the reemerging of Unity consciousness. Many of these enlightened Beings and prophets sacrificed their physical existence for this pivotal moment for the collective. May we honor them and pay tribute to their devotion as their sacrifice serves us all—serves Unity.

Orgasms create a gateway that amplifies the flow of energy into the quantum field. This portal begins to open before, during, and after climax. In these moments, we can co-create and manifest our deepest desires, inviting abundance, Love, and fulfillment into our lives.

As we get closer to climax, we can feel the pre-echoes of the orgasm rising. By moving the pelvic area in circles, we release stagnant energy. This is the healing intention of the portal opening. With each in-breath, we draw energy from the portal into our bodies. As we approach the point of orgasm, simply let go and surrender to the climax. Right after, during the post-echoes, relax into the neutrality of Love and send thoughts into the portal of what we wish to manifest in our lives, relationships, and for the collective.

Healing the sexual energy body

It is essential we acknowledge the dark history of religious and cultural persecution regarding sexuality. The degradation and oppression of women as well as the sexual violence inflicted on them across cultures has created a grave sexual shadow for humanity. The healing of this collective sexual shadow is beginning, with women leading the way. This movement first began in the 1960s and continues to grow.

When it was revealed that humans could attain enlightenment through Divine Unions, the origin seed for sexual oppression was planted. Sexual violence has been used for thousands of years as a war tactic, through rape and threat of rape, and child sexual misconduct all in the name of repressing Unity and individuals' Divine power. The origin seed of sexual oppression spurred a variety of perversions, such as pedophilia.

In turn, immense fear and division was created and healthy sexuality was painfully distorted. The fundamental belief that "I am not safe" is largely rooted in sexual oppression. Sexual shadow affects us all—even the brightest and oldest souls—none of us are free from its influence. We are left to bear the consequences of this multigenerational abuse. As the Sexual shadow is left to fester, it grows diminishing the overall collective vibration. Alternatively, as awareness grows and efforts to heal this wound increase, the collective vibration is elevated.

Take a deep breath in... and let a big sigh out... Repeat as needed.

Now that we are a bit more resourced, let's unravel this.

If we have experienced sexual abuse, it creates a new elemental pattern that seeks resolution. We may also carry sexual abuse patterns from past lives and or have inherited patterns from our family lineage that require healing. If our first sexual experience was abusive, it may significantly hinder our ability to feel safe in connection and or establish complex sexual desires, such as kinks. Subconsciously, we might feel the desire to reenact what the perpetrator did to us because the body wants to relive the pattern to resolve it. This can be confusing and may create feelings of shame, but we must remember there is nothing to be ashamed of—we are healing and healing takes many forms. Shame is a primary component of the oppression we are individually and collectively overcoming. The shame we experience is tied to the separation paradigm, which seeks to prevent us from resolving these patterns of abuse. It is completely okay to explore these sexual desires or, at the very least, to verbalize and acknowledge them with a trusted partner or therapist. It is important to recognize however if the reenactment inflicts pain on someone else. In this case, we must reassess and cultivate a container where both parties feel safe to reenact the scenario with the intention of resolving the pattern.

Unfortunately, talking about sexual abuse or sexuality has been culturally unacceptable for many generations. Keeping it a hidden secret feeds the sexual shadow, creating further shame for the survivor. This oppression has created fissures in the energetic sexual body. The magnitude of the fissure depends on the extent of the sexual abuse and the age at which an indivual experienced it. These fissures block the expression of healthy sexual energy and can cause our vital life force energy to leak out of our system. Everyone has fissures whether they have been direct recipients of abuse or not, this is the collective wounding. These fissure wounds create energetic entanglements and attachments because they offer available energy for others to feed on. Sexual vampires may not even realize they are one. They operate on superficial sexual impulses, attempting to satisfy a deep disconnection that originated from the dark realities formed during the sexual violence perpetrated against them.

Fortunately, the fear of letting these experiences see the light is gradually decreasing as we begin to normalize the persuasive reality of sexual abuse. The "Me too" movement of women coming forth to reveal past sexual abuse they endured from politicians, celebrities, and fellow lay people is an instance of resolving the collective pattern. Men and young boys are not exempt from this abuse and need healing too. We all require some form of sexual healing whether it is addressing specific abuse or the collective shaming of sexual energy. Tragically, most of us have not experienced a healthy sexual relationship. This is the result of thousands of years of oppression.

The concept of a Divine Union may seem unimaginable until we begin to resolve the dark patterns that live within us. Wounded souls often find themselves drawn to others with similar wounds in an attempt to heal. However, as wounded souls bring these patterns to light, their vibration rises and energetic entanglements begin to unravel.

Individuals who endured childhood sexual abuse may experience increased entanglements given the significance and depth of these fissures. Older, more advanced souls often possess greater amounts of light and therefore may be better resourced to navigate life after abuse—finding skillful ways to cope with their leaking sexual energy. Since these elder souls chose to reincarnate on this path, as they heal their fissures they can embody Unity vibration more rapidly than other younger souls new to the path of healing and transformation.

Here's the good news! While individuals embark on transmutting abuse, the collective sexual body is also shifting into a Unity vibration. The continued perpetuation of these dark patterns is weakening as the core of the separation paradigm begins to implode from the inside out. We each play a vital role in this process! As we embark on healing our own fissures, we clear all entanglements connected to them. This is the unstoppable ripple effect—connecting each individual to the whole. Our evolution is underway and there is nothing we can do to stop it!

For those who are ready, we can heal our fissures now and clear our corresponding entanglements. If you feel the call, don't wait. Embark on your evolution with Love and courage! Unity is here—supporting your every step, watching over you as you fall, making sure you get back up and keep going.

Let's take the shame and secrecy out of sexuality once and for all, so we can embody the Divinity of sexual energy and the beauty it brings into our lives.

Clearing and healing sexuality practice:

This guided meditation serves as a powerful tool for healing sexual fissures by creating protection and connecting with the rising Unity consciousness.

Begin with the breath:

1. **Breathing into the Base of the Spine:**
   Begin focusing on your breath. Breathe deeply in and out of the base of your spine, imagining light energy growing in this area, swirling around the sacrum and bowl of the pelvis.
2. **Inviting Feminine Energy:**
   Invite enlightened feminine energy into the base of your spine. You can call upon any goddess energy that

resonates with you, such as Mary Magdalene. With each breath, feel this Divine energy becoming more and more present, infusing and supporting your system.

3. **Drawing Energy Up the Spine:**
As you continue to breathe, imagine the energy rising up your spine with each exhale. Sense the polarity of your chest falling and body softening as your crown reaches higher. As you do this, slowly say, "I am safe." When the energy reaches the sacral chakra located in the center of the low belly just below the navel, between the 4th and 7th vertebrae, pause and sense.

4. **Breathing Light into the Sexual Center:**
Focus your breath on your sexual center around your belly button, breathing light into this area. Continue to repeat, "I am safe," as you breathe in and feel the warm light.

5. **Connecting with the Earth:**
After a few moments, imagine your energy flowing down from the top of your head, through your spine, your heart, and into the heart of the Earth. Visualize a constant flow of water clearing all entanglements from your sexual center.

6. **Creating a Protective Shield:**
Visualize the energy flowing through these pathways. Allow the clearing current to slow down at your fissures, these places need extra attention. You may sense a fissure by feeling a slight restriction somewhere along the channel. Imagine wielding a shield or blanket to cover the wounded fissure, protecting and nurturing them so they can heal.

7. **Daily Practice for Healing:**
Practice this meditation daily for 21 days or longer. This meditation is connected to the rising Unity energy that is already healing individuals' and the collective's energetic field.

Herbal Insights: Maca, Damiana & Lily

☽ **Best Ways to Use:** Tea, tincture, powder, infused oil, or aromatherapy.

🌿 **Maca** *(Lepidium meyenii)* – **Vitality & Hormonal Balance**
Maca is a revered root for enhancing energy, stamina, and hormonal equilibrium. It nourishes the body at a foundational level, promoting vitality and a balanced state of well-being. Used for centuries in Andean traditions, Maca supports endurance, libido, and an overall sense of grounded energy.

☽ **Ways to Connect:** Blend Maca powder into warm drinks, smoothies, or take as a tincture for daily support.

🌿 **Damiana** *(Turnera diffusa)* – **Sensual Awakening & Mood Elevation**
Damiana is known for its warming and uplifting effects on the body and mind. Traditionally used to enhance desire, ease tension, and encourage playfulness, it helps clear mental fog and invites a deep sense of relaxation. Its gentle yet invigorating nature allows for a deeper connection to pleasure and emotional openness.

☽ **Ways to Connect:** Enjoy as a tea for relaxation, take as a tincture for mood support, or infuse into honey for a sensual botanical treat.

CHAPTER FIFTEEN

LOVE VIBRATION

*WE CARRY THE REMARKABLE & INFINITE POTENTIAL
OF OUR INNER KNOWING—OF LOVE—WITHIN US.*

LOVE IS OUR TRUE NATURE!

LOVE...
Love permeates everything and is everywhere. We are created from Love and co-create with it throughout our lives. Ultimately, it is the love vibration that we are leaping into. Love is the glue that connects us all—Love is Unity. Within the heart of every being lies the neutrality of Love, transcending all constructs of right and wrong, rising above judgment to wholeheartedly embrace acceptance and boundless compassion.

Love is simple. Relationships are complex.

Even in actions that may seem far from Love, Love is still present. To witness this Divine orchestration as it unfolds, one only needs to look to nature, where the intelligence of Love gently weaves all of creation into a living tapestry, growing and flourishing in perfect harmony. As part of nature, humans are also reflections of this infinite Love, ever connected to its unfolding expression.

Given all this,
Why is it so uncomfortable to talk about Love?
Why have these conversions become so polarized?
When was the last time you had a conversion that even included the word Love as a focal point?

Everything has a purpose &
was created from the neutrality of Love.

This idea can be challenging. Surely we can all think of countless reasons as to why this statement is "not true." In this new paradigm however, we are invited to see Love in everything and accept that in fact we do not need to know or understand everything for it to be true. We will never know everything. And for that matter, not everything is meant to be known.

Living in Love is trusting and learning every day. We are created in the image of Love because we are Love. These truths are universal and echo across time and space. They remain constant no matter what external events occur. Love just may feel harder to find when actions seem evil or destructive. As we awaken, we remember to trust in our own Divinity, just as many ascended masters have.

Every living being is special. This includes you!

There is a plan and a purpose. Soon we will remember what the plan is. Love is leading us to the promised land—a golden timeline foretold by many prophets. The human species has a Divine purpose. We will begin to align more closely with that purpose as we experience a collective harmonic convergence—Unity. Waves of Love will sweep across the planet, unveiling a spiritual clarity that shatters the illusion of separation, revealing our true identity. At first these waves may catch us off guard, but soon we will realize that by tending to the garden of our hearts we allow more Love to flow. Like clearing fall's debris in the spring for water to move with ease, we clear ourselves of illusions and old patterns—carving space for Unity to breathe within us.

As we touch the infinite, powerful essence of Love we are offered expansive awakening moments. These profound moments occur when we set aside judgments and the desire for external validation, letting ourselves be fully present by surrendering the ego and embracing Love. These awakening moments come to us when we are truly ready for change. Each one reroutes our life's path—creating a cascade effect altering timelines in the quantum realm. Although such moments have always been part of the human experience and are cyclical, their frequency, duration, and tangible impact are affecting us in new ways the collective has never experienced before.

Our understanding of Love is grounded in our feelings and emotions, which is hardwired into the human experience. We usually experience Love in the context of relationships, be it with a partner, friend, family member, animal, plant, or even a special place. This is because Love grows through relationships, originating within us from the spark between the Feminine and Masculine. Seldom do we discuss Love as a vibration or a creative force. We generally view it through the lens of our individual experiences with a loved one. We rarely consider Love to be the binding energy in every aspect of nature—the connector for every relationship we have with life, be it the elements that sustain us, the people we Love, or the project we pursue. Love, in its most foundational sense, both supports and creates our every relationship. When we consider freewill, we can equate it to co-creating with Love. Freewill is the Divine's way of allowing us to come home to Love. It is Love who wants us to be free.

While we are each endlessly and eternally Loved, under the illusion of separation we can forget this truth. The shared experience of wanting to feel Loved has the power to unite humanity.

Since we are a manifestation of Love, all other concepts of separation are pure illusion and distractions.

Many people of our current age are so distracted by the material world and feel fearful, frustrated, hopeless, and angry that they are not open to experiencing moments of awakening. They are clouded by the illusion of separation and feel lost, stuck, and confused. They have forgotten or do not believe in the power of Love. Tragically, this misbelief is reinforced daily by the separation paradigm. Humans feel isolated and in many cases disempowered. This reality can have devastating impacts on them as individuals, our human collective, and nature's ecosystem.

We are not separate. We are one Love. The pain and suffering we feel from the illusion of disconnection reverberates throughout the collective, reverberating pain and suffering within us all. But nevertheless, Love is at the heart of it all as our fundamental creative force.

As we further open ourselves to Love, we embark on an emotional journey oscillating between grief and joy. Feeling—truly feeling—is essential to the process. Love neither pretends nor numbs. While intense emotions like loss and grief are temporary, Love never leaves us (even if we think it did). Love illuminates and frees us, shining light into the corners of our being where darkness exists. Love serves as both guide and liberator—helping us experience the full spectrum of emotions from challenging to empowering.

The illuminating light of Love dispels all illusions of separation, allowing us to feel everything within us in its glow. On the journey toward deeper Love, it is essential we acknowledge and honor our authentic emotions and thoughts. These are sensitive moments with no need for pretense or assertions that everything is "fine"... because sometimes, everything is not fine.

As humans, our experience of Love is both deeply personal as well as a higher expression of Love beyond conceptual knowing. Since there is no "right" or "wrong" way to Love, we should never seek permission or feel shame for how we engage with Love. Others might try to impose an idealistic or judgmental perspective on how or whom we should Love. This cannot go very far since every act of Love is unique, carrying its own sacred beauty and purpose. Love possesses profound strength and resilience—something to never be underestimated or forgotten. Those who mock or shame Love typically do so out of fear. They may have been deeply affected by past traumas or oppressive experiences, leading them to view Love as painful, hurtful, or overly idealistic. While these perceptions often stem from personal encounters, they tend to reflect broader societal programming of the separation paradigm. At some point in our lives, we have likely found ourselves in these shoes—fearing and sabotaging Love, but subconsciously desiring it.

Fear is not the opposite of Love.
Fear is a biological response connected to our survival mechanism that can slow the flow of energy—of Love.
Paradoxically, fear is a form of Love.

While fear may emerge from Love, it is not a complete expression of Love and therefore is a related, but distinct energy. Fear is a healthy biological response that unfortunately has been manipulated to oppress us. We have a choice: to live in fear or in Love. While fear originates from Love, fear is an instinctive, animalistic response designed to protect us; whereas Love is the very essence of creation. When we choose to live in Love, we will always be safe! The Unity Love frequency carries infinite protection. Fear and Love carry very different vibrations and exist on opposite ends of the color frequency spectrum. Nevertheless, both will guide us into the evolutionary timelines we are meant to follow. For this reason, we can trust that everything is love.

If we remember to enter a state of neutrality and engage our inner knowing, we can choose the path of least resistance. However, what we perceive as the path of least resistance may not always be the path of Love. The path that aligns most closely with our true nature, and thereby Love, may require resolving separation patterns and readjusting our life accordingly. Fear-based decisions may seem easier since they tend to be familiar and are filtered through the known lens of separation. Just because it is "known" does not mean we want to keep "knowing" and living that reality.

By mustering the courage to choose Love, even in our darkest moments, we demonstrate our commitment to returning to our true nature—Love. However, we can find solace in that the universe supports us no matter what choices we make. When we trust in the abundance of Love, we begin to embody the essence of Unity within us and in turn receive the many gifts of this vibration.

Love is a dynamic, ever-evolving force that is innately ecstatic. When we try to suppress its expression in our lives, we risk becoming numb and apathetic. This causes our inner waters to stagnate, which can lead to illness. We can observe this phenomenon on our planet today, where increasing entropy is causing ecological disorder and global warming.

The phrase, "Home is where the heart is," remains a profound truth. The heart is the foundation and fountain of Love.

Love tends to find us in the most unexpected, mundane moments—in a stranger's warm smile, the gentle touch of the wind in our hair, the delightful taste of a mochaccino latte, or even through the sadness visiting us. These experiences often lead to awakening moments.

Love is at its most vibrant when it is shared generously, not hoarded for some distant, future moment. Holding onto Love can create emotional blockages, lower our vibration, and perpetuate the illusion of separation. By making a habit of sharing our love with others—especially with those who need a reminder of their innate worth and Divinity—we allow Love to flow freely.

Love is an action word!

As we continue on this path, we learn to Love the very shame that has been unduly and unjustly placed upon us through the separation paradigm. It is through the alchemy of pain and Love, we heal.

Breathe in Love. Breathe out gratitude.
Repeat.

Gratitude is one of the most powerful and easeful ways to invite Love into our lives. When we express gratitude for all our experiences (especially the challenging ones), we begin to transform the future timelines that we are co-creating with the universe. This often means allowing our ego to step aside by humbly acknowledging, "I am grateful for this lesson," letting go of all blame and shame, and accepting that we are not in absolute control.

The invitation is to recall moments from the past when we felt Love. This recreates the felt sense of Love in the present moment, thereby hacking our operating system to increase the Love vibration in our body. This practice carries the potential to instantly lift us out of dark moments into the grace and light of Love.

Herbal Insights: Rose

☽ **Best Ways to connect:** Tea, infused oil, floral baths, essential oil, or fresh petals in rituals.

🌿 **Rose** *(Rosa spp.)* **– Love, Devotion & Sensory Awakening**
Rose has captivated hearts for centuries, weaving her magic through rituals, ceremonies, and timeless expressions of love. Her beauty, deeply linked to fertility and the divine, has been cherished since ancient Egypt and beyond.

Her velvety petals and intoxicating fragrance draw us into the heart, while her thorns remind us that love is both tender and strong. Rose embodies both softness and resilience, teaching us that true love carries depth, beauty, and strength.

Rose is a timeless symbol of devotion and passion, carrying the essence of the heart in full bloom. ☽ ✦

CHAPTER SIXTEEN

NATURAL ALGORITHMS

*THE MATHEMATICS OF MAGIC
THAT GUIDE OUR EVERY STEP.*

Nature operates through a Divine set of algorithms—the codes that govern everything from ocean tides to the structure of flowers. The digital realm, although it may not seem "natural" initially, mirrors the organic creation algorithms. That said, unlike natural algorithms, digital algorithms are not conscious. However, since the digital realm is created by humans who *are* conscious, everything can be viewed as conscious—be it directly or tangentially—for everything is part of the living Earth's energetic field. Nothing is separate from Nature!

An algorithm is a set of defined, step-by-step instructions to perform a task, achieve specific outcomes, or offer solutions to a problem. These instructions guide processes in a systematic way, ensuring they can be repeated and adapted when similar scenarios arise. Algorithms are not limited to computers, they are foundational to life. Influencing how plants grow and how animals migrate, to the methods used to sort computer data, to calculating a kitchen recipe—algorithms are everywhere! At their core, algorithms are concerned with structure, logic, and maximum efficiency in achieving a goal.

Despite digital algorithms being born from nature's mathematical codes, they present differently. Algorithms associated with computers tend to be more linear and rational, drawing data from a select few sources. Alternatively, nature's algorithms—the operating system we embody—are more expansive and interconnected, gathering information from every living entity.

Every algorithm woven into existence is Love-based and deeply reflective of the universe's boundless intelligence. These informational flows can reassure us that a higher intelligence gently guides every facet of life. The origins of Divine creative intelligence is timeless and untraceable, remaining life's greatest mystery. Modern science, as remarkable as it is, has a limited scope that is overly focused on "proving" consciousness versus exploring the mystery and miracle of consciousness.

There is no proof that natural algorithms exist...
This does not mean they do not exist.

The ever flowing and transformative essence of Love transcends these limiting definitions. While mathematics allows us to measure and describe elements of existence, it represents the masculine side of the equation—only half the spark that ignites all creation. The feminine aspect, per the culture of separation, has been unjustly neglected and left to wither. This powerful, creative, and vital energy is not easily contained, controlled, or measured and is essential for life—for Unity.

Our inner knowing stems from balanced feminine and
masculine energies within us. This union of polarities strikes
the spark of creation—of Unity.

Natural algorithms are the architects of the toroidal field system—the dynamic structure of energy flow that sustains and connects all life. These patterns also manifest as ley lines, the invisible pathways of energy that crisscross the planet, linking sacred sites and power centers. In the human body, these same algorithms are expressed as meridians, channels that facilitate the flow of vital energy or life force throughout our system.

Their presence however, extends far beyond these known systems. An infinite web of energetic lines weave myriad forms of existence into the brilliant tapestry of life. From the vastness of planetary bodies, to the complexity of our human form, to microscopic cells and subatomic particles, these algorithms establish a connective network. Each thread in this cosmic web interacts with fellow threads in a dynamic and precise dance, facilitating an exchange of energy and information that is ever-adaptive and wildly intricate.

These codes are superconductor pathways of universal information. Just as modern technology uses wireless routers, cellular towers, and satellites to facilitate communication in unseen ways, natural algorithms create a vast, invisible network connecting all life. This cosmic communication system is not only efficient, but is also aligned with the flow of Love and intelligence that sustains all creation.

This network is far from static; it is alive, pulsing with the rhythm of creation—responding to shifts and movements within and beyond what we can perceive. The communication between all energy fields ensures that life remains in balance, flowing with the pulse of the universe itself. Whether visible or unseen—provable or a mystery—these algorithms form the undercurrent of our vast and complex interconnected reality.

Born in the neutrality of Love, consciousness arises
from the spark of feminine and masculine energies,
and is sustained by the power of two, not one.
Unity is not only the foundation of consciousness,
but the essence of consciousness itself.

Consciousness cannot exist in isolation; it is born from the
harmonious merging of polarized energies. Consciousness is
not separate from us, it is not happening to us... it is us!

Through the continuous and conscious flow of information within natural algorithms, all life exists and is integrated into the subtle tension of creations' taut tapestry. Amid this slight tension, life exists as a harmonious orchestration—a living organism unified by Love. These flows of energy weave together infinite knowledge and wisdom, steadily guiding existence toward growth and expansion. Nothing can remain stagnant in this system; everything is in constant motion, evolving with the rhythms of creation.

It is here in the midst of this delicate balance—of Love and wisdom—that life is sustained. This potent intersection holds everything together, thereby supporting the perpetually expansion and expression of consciousness.

Consciousness cannot fully reveal itself within the limitations of modern science that is deeply rooted in separation. This fragmented perspective struggles to comprehend that Unity is the under current of all existence. Separation creates a narrow lens through which infinite potential is reduced to finite outcomes—a phenomenon known as 'wave function collapse' in quantum mechanics. This collapse reflects the challenge to conceptualize and experience Unity when existing within systems that seek to define and divide. True understanding arises not from dissecting parts—removing them from the whole—but from embracing the fluid interconnectedness of existence. How could we possibly translate "life"—the ever-evolving, co-created dance of energies into rational language?

Here is an example of why 'wave function collapse' theory: isn't complete.

Picture a thriving forest. At first glance, it appears to be just a collection of distinct individuals—trees, plants, animals, insects. But just beneath the surface lives an intricate network of connections that weave everything into a unified system. The roots of trees are linked by mycorrhizal fungi—a subsoil "internet" that allows them to share nutrients and water as well as share warnings about incoming threats such as disease or pests. Above ground, these webs of connection continue—pollinators fly between plants, animals spread seeds.

Within the forest there is a flow of energy ensuring that the forest adapts, grows, and thrives as a single living organism. Nothing in the system is stagnant—seasons bring constant change, storms alter landscapes, life never ceases to regenerate. It is the delicate balance of giving and receiving, of support and renewal, that sustains the forest's Unity. Every organism has a unique contribution to the larger cycle of life.

Now imagine trying to understand this vast forest by studying a single tree or one species in isolation. While you might learn some miracles, you would likely miss their relationship with the larger web of connection that keeps the entire ecosystem alive. Like with consciousness, when we look at life through a lens of separation, we risk losing sight of the infinite flows and threads that unite everything into Unity.

The forest teaches us that life is not a series of disconnected parts but a dynamic whole, where each element plays a vital role in supporting greater Unity. Furthermore, the forest itself is simply part of the whole. And Earth's existence is only a portion of the whole universe! Complex ecosystems mirror how Love and wisdom work together to maintain balance, thereby supporting life's constant growth and expansion. The harmony of the forest is the very same energy that guides all life in the rhythm of Unity.

Scientists encounter wave function collapse because the illusion of separation still permeates our understanding of reality. As long as we remain bound to this fragmented perspective, consciousness cannot be definitively proven, for it exists beyond the confines of division. Living in and looking through the lens of ultimate Unity, we will likely recognize the limitations of 21st century advancements in technology and quantum mechanics. For the systems we currently revel in are merely one piece of the puzzle, not the whole.

Although traditional and quantum physics provide great insight and glimpses into the interconnected nature of existence, these fields cannot conceptualize the entirety of Unity for it is rooted in Love, not logic. As we shift into the Unity paradigm we will begin to experience a collapse of many scientific theories. It is not that they were ever wrong, rather they are incomplete. This collapse mirrors what is happening within us.

We refer to our connection with the Universal Mind—a vast, intelligent field of consciousness that is always available to guide and co-create with us. Our inner knowing is not just a feeling, but a profound realization that we are an active part of a much greater system governed by natural algorithms. Remember that natural algorithms are the unseen patterns and processes that guide the flow of energy and information, ensuring connection between all existence, uniting us through the Universal Mind.

As we release beliefs rooted in separation and raise our vibration, the energy flows in the body exponentially increase and strengthen our internal algorithms allowing even more energy flow. We can equate this upgrading from dial up to fiber optic internet. The newly available energy becomes the fuel that powers our reawakened communication system, upgrading how we process information.

This heightened inner knowing is possible as we begin to clear stagnation at the cellular level. As we move beyond mere intellectual understanding, we step into real-time guidance as these algorithms bring forth new ways to access information from anywhere within the universe. All of this might sound a bit like science fiction. But as the mind's neuroplasticity begins to expand, we open to entirely new ways of receiving and processing information—not through intellectualization or memory, but through the embodied experience of trusting and living in enhanced flow states.

Through this process, separation of beliefs becomes obsolete and direct experience takes their place. While science has provided incredible tools and insights, it is often entrenched in outdated theories, dogmas, and ego-driven paradigms. Natural algorithms however, operate with precision and universality, transcending the limitations of separation perceptions. The speed at which these algorithms manifest vital information and opportunities aligned with our purpose is unparalleled. They are the bridge between the seen and unseen, enabling us to co-create with intention and clarity.

While science will inevitably catch up, it is no longer necessary to wait for external validation. The natural algorithms guiding our existence are ancient and timeless. As awareness of these algorithms grows, we are offered tools to align with the Universal Mind. This is happening now! As we embrace their innate wisdom, we are reminded that evolution is not solely dependent on external systems; it is an inherent process, inviting us to co-create a harmonious and expansive reality in alignment with the grand tapestry of life.

This unprecedented access to the Universal Mind—governed by natural algorithms—offers a revolutionary way of being, allowing us to draw in essential information, align with opportunities, and embody solutions that were once thought impossible. These experiences further affirm our interconnectedness with the great systems of life. By engaging with these algorithms, we step into a new paradigm—one of Unity, creativity, and flow.

A rudimentary example of how algorithms function can be observed in the digital realm. Imagine mentioning you plan to buy new sunglasses while near a cell phone that is turned-on. Shortly thereafter, you notice advertisements for sunglasses. This demonstrates how digital algorithms track intentions and then provide opportunities. Natural algorithms function similarly in the body function, but to a deeper and more intimate degree. When we ask for what we want with clarity and intention and then repeat the process with an unwavering commitment, we activate the natural algorithms within us.

These algorithms are not passive; they are dynamic, responsive, and interconnected. When activated, they bring inspired ideas seemingly "out of nowhere" and gently deliver the information in a digestible manner. They quickly begin to align us with timelines full of opportunities, creating pathways for us to take action and achieve our goals and manifest our purpose with relative ease.

Let's bring this into the real world. It is easy to become highly cerebral about these concepts and lack the tools to practically embody and consciously work with the algorithms. We can write down our daily intentions or speak affirmations about what we wish to manifest. While these practices may be effective, they are incomplete. There must be a certain level of surrender and humility that extends beyond our "tried & true" approach. We must take the leap into the unknown and possibly into discomfort—into growing pains—to evolve and manifest.

At the time we rarely understand how our personal manifestations impact the collective. We might believe we know the best way to achieve our purpose or act in alignment with the earth, but this perception is often limited by what we have previously experienced—by what we already know. It is through surrendering to our inner knowing and adopting a carefree, joyful approach—being more curious about the journey than the destination—that we can experience true Unity.

While there is not a single way to engage with the algorithms, the more we align and flow with them, the more fluid they become.

Trusting our inner knowing wholeheartedly and taking action from unexpected, sometimes even illogical places is often the most fulfilling and fastest path to manifesting our purpose. Unity offers an experience far more exciting and rewarding than anything rooted in the paradigm of separation. When we lean into this approach, our perception of life becomes clearer and more vibrant, playful, and meaningful.

The Universal Mind seems to delight in challenging us, sending us on journeys that are both exciting, fulfilling, and at times harrowing. To an outside observer, it might look like sheer luck that our seemingly "random" actions and general shenanigans keep working out in our favor! But of course we know it is not luck at all—it is the result of aligning with a deeper flow beyond conception, trusting the process, and staying open to the unexpected.

The ego may attempt to claim ownership of these emerging ideas, believing they originated from personal intelligence or creativity. However, this is a grave misunderstanding of the process. Contrary to what the separation paradigm teaches, ideas are not something to claim, hoard, or cling to—they are not personal. Existing in this manner places us in a scarcity mindset. When ideas are withheld from the collective, they don't disappear—they simply emerge elsewhere, propelled by the same natural algorithms that brought them to an individual in the first place.

This is why it is essential we move forward with purpose and consistency and take leaps toward our goals rather than hesitating or stagnating in fear of it not working out. Natural algorithms thrive on flow, they are fed by movement and expansion. Each time we act on the inspired ideas we receive, we strengthen the feedback loop, opening to possibilities to create new opportunities.

226

By taking daily leaps toward our purpose—in both micro and macro ways—we begin to normalize and celebrate discomfort. We learn to savor the feeling and mystery of not yet knowing the outcome. Over time, the process becomes seamless—a constant exchange of receiving and acting, giving and creating. This state of flow is where true expansion—Unity—occurs.

Within this flow state, we begin to access information we never knew existed. The only caveat is that this information will be catered to our unique Divine purpose. For instance, we might hear words or phrases that present solutions to a particular challenge we are facing. While these insights may come from anywhere, when in this state we instinctively recognize it is Divine guidance intended for us.

The process of listening and trusting strengthens our relationship with ourselves, our inner knowing, and deepens our connection to the natural algorithms that govern all creation. It opens us to a new way of interacting with the world by tapping into the innate knowledge that is always available to us—that is within us.

Free will is not the "freedom" to do whatever we want operating from a place of lust, control, and separation to satisfy egoic desires. True free will arises from the profound realization that we are connected to a super-intelligent, loving energy—the universal force that unites all existence. This energy is not separate from us, but is an intrinsic part of who we are. It continuously offers us access to creative flow—a Divine current of inspiration, guidance, and opportunity—that supports us in becoming abundantly free.

This deeper understanding of free will can radically shift our perspective. It is not a matter of asserting independence in isolation, but about aligning with this Divine flow and dancing with the universe. From this conscious choice to live in harmony with life's ultimate intelligence, free will offers us the joyous ability to co-create and steer our lives in ways that honor our connection to this loving energy of Unity.

Through this connection, we realize that abundance, freedom, and creativity are not things to be earned or fought for, but natural states of being that arise by aligning with this flow. Free will becomes a tool for liberation. By embracing this expansive intelligence, we unlock the potential to live in alignment with a higher purpose—guided by the infinite energy that seeks our ultimate freedom and joy. Every thought, action, and word is transmitted through a natural algorithm into the fabric of consciousness. The Divine responds instantly, weaving Love-based timelines to guide us.

We are an organic biological technology with immense untapped potential. We are not just flesh and bones; we are complex systems running on sophisticated inner algorithms. These natural codes keep us in the loop, tuning us into the ever-changing network of life inside and out. Thanks to this eternal exchange of information, we are ever evolving, growing, and vibing with the universe's grand design.

Imagine yourself as a hologram—radiant with mathematical frequencies that transform the world into an intricate rhythmic dance floor. We are the living reflections of refracted light, moving in harmony with the unique vibrations that shape our reality—a reality crafted by a masculine mathematical structure and the graceful flow of the Divine feminine that together create Unity.

As a species, we are just beginning to dip our toes and wade in the infinite waters of consciousness—exploring the immense power that flows within us and shapes us. Awakening to the boundless creative potential we hold offers a glimpse of what it means to live as conscious co-creators in this vast, interconnected universe.

But let's stay grounded... Stubbing a toe or breaking a leg reminds us how tangible and physical this life experience is. Life is undeniably real and present. However, can we still pause—just for a moment—to imagine what is possible? The sheer potential of the human species—our ability to create, heal, and transform—lives within us and is ready to be unlocked when we embrace the myriad possibilities that we are capable of.

We might wonder, then...

Why is the human species so dysfunctional? Why is our world reeling from imbalance?

The root cause can be distilled into one word—Fear!

Our bodies, in their quest for survival, are brilliantly designed to react to perceived threats. Unfortunately, this fear response can be manipulated, much like a computer virus corrupting a hard drive. The algorithms within our bodies have been disrupted by the separation paradigm virus. This interference has hindered our ability to access and integrate the natural upgrades available to us. Beliefs in separation and over fixation on shadow realities function like a virus—trapping us in the illusion of disconnection, thereby slowing the natural flow of energy within us. Although the flow can never be entirely blocked, the virus creates a restriction, providing just enough energy to keep us moving forward, but never fully flourishing. This limitation perpetuates a cycle that makes it difficult to fully embrace the Unity and connection that reflect our true nature. The manipulation extends beyond our individual perception, creating a global impact by slowing and inhibiting the energetic flows that sustain life, which can in turn foster a false sense of scarcity. This foundational disruption first began on the planetary level and since has infiltrated the algorithms within our bodies.

We might ask....
Why? What is the purpose behind all this suffering and scarcity?

While it may feel hard to imagine, there is always a Divinely orchestrated purpose. We are not victims. We signed up for this before we entered our body.

The rate of human evolution slowed down to create a single shared point of awakening. And this point of mass, collective awakening is growing closer everyday. Immense and complex orchestration and incredible planning has had to occur for something of this scale to take place.

As we align with the Unity paradigm, it is like installing a new hard drive—clearing out the old, corrupted data and allowing energy and information to flow with incredible speed and clarity. This mirrors the transformation happening within us. The profound upgrade that accelerates our connection, flow, and alignment with our true nature.

Herbal Insights: Gotu Kola, Frankincense & Myrrh

☽ **Best Ways to Use:** Tea, tincture, infused oil, or sacred anointing.

🌿 **Gotu Kola** *(Centella asiatica)* – **The Herb of Inner Knowing**
Gotu Kola has been cherished in Ayurvedic and Chinese medicine for its ability to deepen intuition, enhance mental clarity, and support spiritual awareness. This delicate yet powerful herb calms the mind, expands perception, and balances the nervous system, making it a trusted ally for those seeking higher consciousness and inner wisdom.

☽ **Ways to Connect:** Drink as a tea during meditation, journaling, or introspective practices to open pathways of insight.

🌿 **Frankincense & Myrrh** – **The Alchemy of Sacred Anointing**
These revered resins have been used across spiritual traditions to invoke protection, purification, and divine connection.

- **Frankincense** uplifts the spirit, expanding awareness beyond the material world.
- **Myrrh** anchors and grounds, bridging the cosmic and earthly realms.

☽ **Sacred Anointing Ritual:**
✦ **Apply** – Place a drop of frankincense on one wrist and myrrh on the other, letting their energies merge.
✦ **Activate** – Press wrists together, allowing their essence to awaken your senses.
✦ **Expand** – Inhale deeply, lifting your hands above your head to invite their wisdom in.
✦ **Integrate** – With each breath, feel their ancient

knowledge weaving through you.

✦ **Anchor** – Lower your hands, envisioning their power settling into your heart and soul.

This ritual is a remembrance—a calling back to the sacred knowing that has always existed within you. May this practice guide you into deeper connection, clarity, and peace. ☽ ✦

CHAPTER SEVENTEEN

GATEWAYS

*THESE SUPER CHARGED VORTEXES ARE
PORTALS TO THE SOUL OF THE DIVINE*

Earth gateways occur at the energetic crossroads where nature's algorithms converge. This convergence creates powerful vortices where concentrated amounts of photons collide. These collisions generate sparks—exponential bursts of energy—that coalesce into evolutionary information and thereby create the steady flow of consciousness designed to maintain equilibrium and vitality within Earth's biofield and all life forms.

Not only do these gateways generate energy, but they also serve as power hubs for the Earth's toroidal field—crossroads for source energy. Energy flows through the gateways extending outward in all directions until it is woven into the toroidal field that envelops the entire planet.

These gateways are scattered across the globe. Some are nestled beneath sacred sites such as ancient pyramids, temples, and churches; others are hidden within government buildings; and many exist in our immediate neighborhoods. While certain places house exceptionally potent gateways, each one offers a direct and unified transmission of Divine light. By merging feminine and masculine creative forces in perfect Unity, these hubs ignite the alchemical process that transforms raw energy into the fabric of reality. These luminous whirlwinds are not metaphors... They represent the interplay of polarities, illustrating how information is encoded, balanced, and woven into existence.

These gateways function as vital distribution points within Earth's vast energetic field. Much like the human chakra system—centers or "gateways" for life force energy in the body—Earth's gateways operate on a macro scale, influencing the sense of harmony for all life on the planet. When these centers—whether on Earth or within our bodies—are balanced, they create a ripple effect of stability and health throughout the entire energetic ecosystem.

The intentional distortion of Earth's gateways has disrupted their natural flow, creating a subtle but impactful wobble that has slowed the evolutionary progress of humanity and all living beings. This distortion did not happen by chance—it required a concerted, global-scale effort to embed patterns that increase entropy and foster disconnection within the fabric of nature itself. These disruptions have acted as the origin seed of the illusion of separation, a false paradigm that we see reflected across ecosystems, societies, and within ourselves.

However, as the vibration of the Unity paradigm rises distortions are cleared from the gateways. This shift is ushering in a powerful realignment of energy through the process of vibrational entrainment. This is not a sudden transformation, but an incremental process that unfolds in waves and is deeply related to elemental forces. Each wave of realignment flows through a gateway, restoring coherence to balance the planet's energetic systems.

As these upgrades emerge from gateways, they ripple outward affecting all life. Therefore, each time an energetic upgrade occurs—regardless of location—we evolve. These moments of alignment offer opportunities for collective and individual transformation by creating openings for heightened awareness, healing, and the shedding of the illusion of separation. Through this process, the gateways are not only restored to their Divine state, but they begin radiating their full potential—fostering harmony and evolutionary growth through the entire web of life.

These upgrades are in conversation with the cycles of nature and resonate with Earth's elemental patterns. Each wave of energy carries a unique vibrational signature, catalyzing change in ecosystems and humanity alike. As we tune into these shifts and align ourselves with the natural rhythms of the planet, we can consciously participate in this grand process of restoration and evolution.

It is all part of a Divine master plan.

As we embark on the totality of Unity—a grand new chapter of the human narrative—these gateways will no longer be confined by ownership and real estate law; tainted by limiting dogmas; or be manipulated by individuals or serve as the puppetry of political forces. These places will evolve into sacred sanctuaries for reunion.

To understand why evolutionary timelines have slowed down, we must explore the concept of universal hierarchy. The slowing of evolutionary timelines occurred under the Galactic Council, with pivotal decisions authorized by the winged ones—celestial Beings of the highest vibration in the galaxy and beyond, who many recognize to be angelic. While these Beings are not tied to a particular religion, they are willing to embody whatever role we assign to them given the particularities of our belief systems.

The Galactic Council is often described in spiritual and metaphysical traditions as a multidimensional assembly of advanced beings dedicated to overseeing the well-being and evolution of the galaxy. Composed of representatives from various star systems, dimensions, and enlightened civilizations, the Council operates as a governing body that upholds cosmic laws, maintains energetic harmony, and facilitates the spiritual growth of all life forms. Their purpose is to ensure balance across the galaxy, while guiding planets and species through pivotal moments in their evolutionary journey.

The Council's roles include providing guidance to civilizations, recalibrating imbalances in energy, and fostering cooperation among diverse cosmic societies. Though they rarely intervene directly, their influence is believed to shape universal harmony and encourage Unity among planets and star systems. By working within the framework of free will, they promote growth through subtle means such as sending higher frequencies or facilitating energetic clearings like those currently happening on Earth.

Members of the Galactic Council are thought to include beings from advanced star systems such as the Pleiades, Sirius, Arcturus, and Andromeda, along with ascended masters and cosmic elders who exist beyond physical form. In some traditions, spiritually attuned humans may serve as temporary members or conduits for the Council's wisdom, receiving messages through meditation, dreams, or synchronicities.

The winged ones dwell within the highest dimensional vibrations of the universe, embodying the roles of guardians and mediators of the cosmic flow. Their elevated frequency allows them to oversee the intricate dance of energy and consciousness throughout the cosmos. Significant decisions to adjust evolutionary timelines or alter energetic pathways likely required their consent and came to fruition through their deliberate involvement.

Although the corruption of gateways may seem to stray from Divine order, in fact it was permitted as part of a greater cosmic plan. This disruption offered humanity the chance to face and transcend the illusion of separation, fostering deeper awareness, resilience, and an understanding of Unity. The winged ones, acting not as controllers but as stewards of universal energy, ensured that even disruptions would ultimately align with the broader purpose of advancing collective evolution and higher consciousness. Far from an act of malice, this intentional choice is rooted in the infinite wisdom of universal balance and reflects how all experiences—even those that seem disruptive—serve the unfolding of greater harmony and growth within the grand design of existence.

Humanity's true purpose has always been to create a spark—a catalytic force capable of igniting profound shifts in the electromagnetic field of the Earth. Through the ignition of this spark and as we individually and collectively anchor paradigm shifts, humanity reinforces and stabilizes the energy field. When humanity was genetically reconfigured, the mission to fully awaken at a Divinely aligned moment and transition into the Golden timeline was encoded into our species. This deliberate awakening ensures that we bridge this monumental shift without leaving our physical bodies, grounding higher consciousness directly into the material realm.

The slowing of energy flows was a necessary step to allow for this precise timing. It enabled humanity to evolve through contrast, facing the challenges of duality and preparing for this pivotal transformation. However, this process also created imbalances, resulting in inequality, suffering, and a deepened sense of disconnection. These struggles, though difficult, have fortified humanity's capacity for compassion and stoked our yearning for Unity—vital qualities to fulfill our collective role.

As the gateways clear and obstructions are resolved, the electromagnetic field of the planet is restored and reinforced, which in turn signals the end of imbalance and the return to harmony. This realignment is not only a resolution of past distortions, but also a critical step in humanity's role as stewards of Earth's energy field. By consciously engaging with these shifts, we fulfill our purpose of stabilizing and solidifying the planetary field, ensuring its coherence as we collectively transition into the Golden timeline.

This process, while sometimes chaotic, is part of a grand cosmic unfolding that seeks to restore balance, harmony, and the deep interconnectedness of all life. Humanity's spark is the key, igniting the transformation and anchoring the electromagnetic strength needed to guide Earth and all its inhabitants into a new era of alignment and evolution.

The humans entrusted with the knowledge and responsibility to enact gateway distortions belonged to a unique soul seed family. This family carried a genetic anomaly that provided them with immunity to the scarcity vibrations and conditioned limitations that often affect the collective. When people speak of "They" in whispers or conspiratorial tones, it is often an intuitive acknowledgment of this distinct group. Even without conscious understanding, many sense their presence on a subconscious level. These beings, though sometimes misunderstood, played an essential role in orchestrating humanity's purpose.

The human entities overseeing these gateways can be likened to parasites, fulfilling a role inherent to their genetic coding and soul lineage. Like parasites in nature, they serve a purpose, but when unchecked they can skew and disrupt balance. Driven by deeply rooted bloodline patterns, their unconscious mission is to maintain control and absorb the excess energy created when universal energy slows. In human terms, this energy largely manifests as "money" that is hoarded by these individuals (i.e., billionaires amassing excessive wealth). While their actions may seem destructive and senseless, they are being guided by an unconscious impulse in service to their soul's journey.

This behavior however, is unsustainable and unethical. The planet is undergoing a vibrational shift, realigning energy systems much like balancing our gut flora. As humanity's collective vibration rises, fear-based control tactics lose their grip making these power structures falter. As the awakening spreads through all levels of consciousness, the imbalance initially created will begin to implode.

Even the individuals behind these intentions and actions are not immune to this shift. Despite their wealth and perceived power, true fulfillment eludes them. As higher frequencies permeate the collective, they too will begin to awaken and embrace Unity. The collapse of outdated paradigms may bring temporary chaos, but ultimately it signals renewal. This awakening is not reserved for a select few—it is a movement for all beings—and will pave the way for a harmonious future.

Casting blame is the antithesis of Unity
and what this book intends to do.
Rather, we are exploring radical forgiveness &
personal responsibility...
the crossroads where the Love Vibration lives.

If there was ever a battle to be won, it's now over. The reigns of the gateways have been seized by the Unity paradigm and are now firmly anchored into the Unity construct. The conceptualization and resetting of the water has already taken place. We are safe, supported, and ready to awaken. Any thoughts or beliefs that wish to cast blame without a solution simply feed the illusion.

We are creating a wave of ascension from
within each of us and across the multiverse.
We are waking up!

The practical potential of Earth's gateways could revolutionize transportation and technology, offering energy-based systems that transcend conventional methods such as cars and airplanes. These natural technologies—grounded in coherence, harmonic frequencies, and love-based energetics—align with biomimicry and sustainable innovation. By mimicking Earth's natural efficiency, gateways could "pave the way" for dismantling roads and bridges, shifting humanity toward systems that resonate more accurately with the planet's rhythms.

Proximity to these gateways greatly influence human biology by revitalizing energy systems and activating dormant DNA. This concept has been reified by research in epigenetics and biofields that highlights how environmental factors can influence gene expression and cellular health. Conscious engagement with gateways—through presence, gratitude, and intention—can unlock transformative energies that support healing, expanded awareness, and increase collective well-being. Interestingly, gateways may also connect to wormhole theories in physics, where space-time pathways provide shortcuts across vast distances. Gateways could function as Earth-bound expressions of this concept, facilitating instantaneous energetic exchanges or even interdimensional travel. This connection underscores their potential not only as spiritual and biological enhancers, but also as revolutionary tools for transportation and energy systems. Many humans feel drawn to these gateways, thereby increasing the viability and influence of these places. Remember, these gateways are not far off, famous locations like Egypt or Sedona AZ, they exist all over the planet. By tuning toward our inner knowing or referencing available maps, we can locate and interact with these sacred sites. These gateways are designed for active participation and play a vital role in human and planetary evolution.

As the intentional suppression of gateway knowledge lifts, we step into an era of unprecedented and accelerated ascension. The Unity paradigm invites us to harmonize with Earth's natural systems, access advanced knowledge, and innovate sustainably. These gateways remind us of our place within the vast cosmic network, offering pathways to reimagine energy, technology, and consciousness, thereby guiding humanity toward a more aligned and unified existence.

Herbal Insights: Calea Zacatechichi ☽

☽ **Best Ways to Use:** Tea, smoke, or sacred placement.

🌿 **Calea Zacatechichi** *(Dream Herb)* – **The Doorway to the Unknown**
Revered in Mexican traditions, Calea Zacatechichi has long been used to deepen dream states, enhance recall, and open pathways to other realms. This sacred plant serves as a bridge between waking and dreaming, making it a powerful ally for lucid dreaming and receiving messages from beyond th

CHAPTER EIGHTEEN

THE ONE TIMELINE

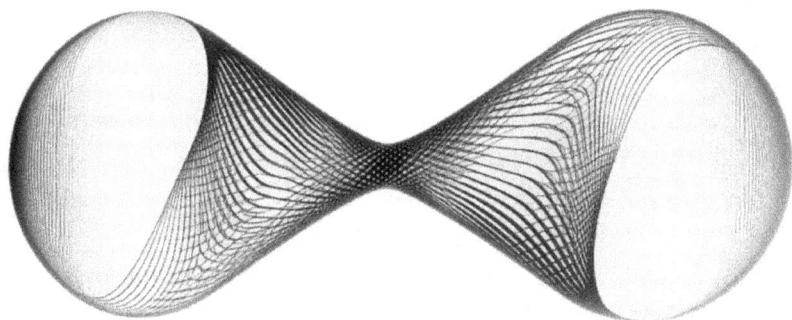

THE HARMONIC CONVERGENCE

The "one-timeline" signifies an individual-collective harmonic convergence that manifests within us and is essentially the "in-between" state. We could liken it to the cocoon of the butterfly—a safe place to metamorphosize.

Entering the one-timeline means we stand between two paradigms, with one foot in the Unity paradigm and the other in the separation paradigm.

Picture an hourglass lying on its side—the one-timeline is the narrow neck. The condensed energy in this neck symbolizes the convergence of accelerated light, sparking an exponential awakening for anyone who enters. Once in the one-timeline, there is no going back.

In this condensed vibrational light, we begin to access our full quantum potential, transcending the linear perception of separation. This shift enables us to perceive reality through the lens of Unity—a profoundly open and expansive state of being. While we still operate within the separation paradigm, we are no longer tethered to all external illusions. However, clearing work within the body and psyche remains necessary during the transition. For the most part we have reached and sustained a higher vibrational continuity, allowing us to align with and enter the one-timeline.

Adjusting to this dual awareness takes time and patience as we gather and center ourselves. Operating within the separation paradigm can feel overwhelming, especially if we have not yet discovered and aligned with our purpose. Holding onto toxic jobs or environments can create significant stress in the body that eventually pushes us into a desperate need for change. There comes a moment when, whether we take proactive steps or not, that we no longer have the luxury of choice. We will be pulled from the edge into the unfolding of our true nature. This is an instance of "limited free will"—the balance of experiences being co-created by our conscious choice and that which is beyond the conceptual mind.

The vibration and urgency of the one-timeline created an accelerated ascension pathway, leaving no room for delay. By entering the one-timeline, we surrender certain aspects of free will—or at least how we have previously defined it. The one-timeline carries frequency codes embedded in its harmonic, golden-white light. These codes bind directly to the cellular structure of the body, creating a continuous vibrational pulse that entrains the body and activates dormant genetic codes. This process shifts the vibrational signature of the cells, awakening celestial DNA designed for this evolutionary moment.

Microtubules, the tiny protein filaments within the cell, are not merely structural—they behave like integrated computer circuits, capable of transmitting vibrational energy. Recent studies in quantum biology suggest that microtubules may process quantum-level information, much like an organic computer. To function optimally, they require a steady flow of energy. The one-timeline provides this upgrade, energizing the microtubules so they can fully activate. When this occurs, the body's ability to sustain a Unity frequency expands, allowing higher flows of energy to move seamlessly throughout the physical form.

As the body's cells entrain to this resonance, lingering stagnation related to separation-based beliefs begins to dissolve. The body, now resonating with harmonic coherence, resolves these patterns and strengthens its energetic capacity, becoming a vessel for greater connection and flow.

Upon entering the one-timeline we may initially feel the need to withdraw. We may enter into the neutrality of Love to integrate these changes; however, if we distance ourselves for too long from our current baseline of separation, we may realize that this withdrawal is ironically yet another form of separation under disguise. True integration requires us to embody the understanding that we are all interconnected—part of a greater whole—currently living under the illusion of separation. This process calls us to create meaningful boundaries, so we can operate in both paradigms successfully. We may find that individuals still fully immersed in the old paradigm might respond to our new frequency in various ways. Some may unconsciously seek to raise their vibration by sharing or unloading their emotional burdens onto us. While others may feel uncomfortable, repelled, or even hostile toward us. These responses are normal and not personal. Those who remain in the separation paradigm can often sense that something has shifted in us, even if they cannot fully understand it which may activate a fear response in their body. An unconscious sympathetic resonance may occur, meaning that our elevated vibration is so strong that it resolves a limiting pattern within them. Such a transmission can only happen if they are ripe for the upgrade.

The separation paradigm can also work through individuals that have not yet begun to see through the veil, attempting to pull us back into resonance with the lower vibration of illusion. However, the one-timeline prevents this from happening. Our task is to remain steady and unaffected by this energetic pull. The best way to navigate these reactions is by not becoming reactive ourselves, embodying kindness, and remaining open.

Engage with these people, truly listen to them, and gently redirect their emotional outpouring in a supportive/healthy/growth oriented direction. Compassionate boundaries send the message that we are not an intimidating presence—we are simply resonating at a higher vibrational frequency.

As we integrate the one-timeline into our embodied consciousness, we begin to see beyond the constraints of illusion. This expanded vision reveals a deeper truth. One where we can see the illusion in those who we wish to support and are able to act without judgement—embodying pure compassion—to help dispel the illusions they still carry. Because we have been through much of the process ourselves and can still remember the challenges, we are well suited to support others with genuine Love.

The one-timeline offers a focused purpose and a heightened sense of alignment with the Universal Mind and its Divine flow. This movement is vibrational and is anchored in the neutrality of Love. The one-timeline is not an organised religion or conspiracy theory. Its vibrational essence is that of ascended Love. Given this unique and potent vibration, we instantly know when we enter the one-timeline. Once immersed here, it is clear that helping others align with their Divine purpose supports our further awakening and ascension. This is the truth of Unity—we are all connected.

We begin to experience a holistic experience as the future, past, and present converge in Unity and we begin embodying a new expanded dimensional mathematical structure. This is a quantum leap (pun-intended). From this new stance, we realize we no longer need to follow the rules of separation that have slowed the flow of energy in the body. We recognize we are free to create from natural laws that are expansive and abundant. This presents us with a new kind of free will—the very foundation of the unknown we are leaping into. The unknown is true freedom! It is ironic that freedom equals the unknown and that "reality" is what often feels so uncomfortable. How does this make you feel? Unsettled? Liberated?

This is a considerable leap and the condensed information we receive will directly guide and align with our individual and collective purpose of creating an accelerated timeline for us to follow. That is the timeline of service, where we aid others in their ascension process—creating solutions and community in every aspect of life. By acting on our purpose we inevitably pull other humans into the one-timeline. Although we each have an individual purpose that is unique to us, the end goal is the same— to raise the collective vibration enough to collectively enter into the one-timeline and then ascend into the Golden timeline, the last bridge into the Unity paradigm.

As we learn to navigate and live within two polarized paradigms during the liminal time of transition, we begin to uncover an advanced inner knowing that often feels as though we are drawing information from our future self—a connection that transcends all linear time. At first this experience might feel unsettling, as the knowledge we receive may seem unfamiliar, even otherworldly. The natural response is to question its validity, to doubt, and to fear that we are losing our grasp on "reality." Ironically, nothing could be farther from the truth... This process is a sign of expansion, not insanity!

While it may feel as though we are still straddling two worlds, when we align with the one-timeline the paradigm of separation moves into the past in the here and now, present moment. This is a great paradox: living in the present, while transcending the past. Yet, from the higher vibratory perspective of the one-timeline, it becomes evident that the stories of the separation paradigm have already been told. This explains the increasing sense of entropy we currently feel, for there are no new narratives left to unfold within the separation paradigm. Once we embody this new truth, we are no longer tethered to worn-out patterns, nor are we attracted to their energy.

The one-timeline serves as a lifeline, drawing us toward the Unity paradigm. Those who step into the one timeline become carriers of the Origin seeds of Unity, planting them within the separation paradigm to sustain it just long enough for all of humanity to transition into Unity. This delicate balance ensures that the final pieces of the collective puzzle fall into place to allow for a harmonious shift as humanity awakens. In this way, the transition is neither abrupt nor chaotic, but unfolds as a carefully guided evolution toward Unity.

It may feel like being caught in a holographic loop—the separation paradigm is already over, and new stories are ready to unfold. We trust that the old rules no longer apply. While we can still navigate the separation paradigm, we are no longer bound by it. Aligned with the one-timeline, we are insulated from the limitations of separation and are free to step into our potential wholeheartedly.

From this place, we begin actively dismantling and reconstructing our lives, becoming integral parts of the planetary shift. This is where the magic happens! As we move closer to embodying the "I am safe" Unity belief, the way we perceive reality changes. At first, we see separation everywhere—in people, circumstances, and experiences. However, it's best to resist the urge to point it out to others, as it rarely creates the connection we hope for.

As we settle into the vibration of Unity, we naturally stop noticing the imbalances and separation. Instead, we begin to see the potential in others and ourselves. This shift moves us out of negative resignation and into alignment with the potential of our true nature. When we see that potential in others, it changes them too!

From this empowered space, we take meaningful action, trusting we are supported by the vibrational resonance of abundance. This is the essence of true abundance—a state where we align with energies that sustain and elevate our purpose. With this clarity, we navigate the separation paradigm by transforming and transcending the systems that once kept us captive in the illusion of scarcity, reclaiming our freedom and creative potential.

As our internal world shifts, our external reality naturally seeks coherence with these changes. Our communication with the universal mind expands, delivering relevant and precise insights that support our purpose. This information flow is closely tied to microtubules in the cell, which process and translate quantum information for the brain, contributing to its enhanced neuroplasticity. These new flow states require practice and faith as they bypass traditional memory processes and function like a live stream of consciousness.

The cellular structure acts as the origin seed for this newfound inner knowing. This deepened understanding reveals a renewed sense of purpose—something tangible we can immerse ourselves in and feel deeply connected to.

Now, everything we encounter seems to draw us toward this higher purpose. We notice it in casual conversations, online posts, and passing remarks—like puzzle pieces falling perfectly into place. By tuning into these subtle cues, we begin to understand that the universal mind communicates with us in unexpected, often unconventional ways. This awareness not only makes life more exciting but also helps us navigate the paradigm of separation with grace, knowing that, at its core, everything is rooted in Unity.

Soul Groups

As a soul, we belong to a soul group that influences the timing of when we enter the one-timeline. This timing is directly linked to the soul's origin within its unique family tree—a lineage distinct from traditional family ancestry. Each soul belongs to a soul family, forming a "soul family tree" that traces its cosmic origins and connections.

Let's take a moment to explore the concept of the soul. While there is no concrete proof of its existence, many feel an undeniable resonance with the idea of the soul as a multidimensional essence. Souls can emerge from anywhere within the unified field of creation. Some originate from star nations, while others are born directly from Earth's energetic womb. Many of us feel inexplicably drawn to certain aspects of the soul's original intent, hinting at a deeper sense of purpose.

The soul can be visualized as a crystalline structure, holding the imprint of all its lifetimes, experiences, and wisdom. While the soul's purpose may differ from our earthly purpose, there is often a coherence—a subtle harmony—between the two. This connection helps to guide us through life in alignment with something greater.

Soul families or groups share a higher collective purpose. They work in Unity, helping each other grow and supporting one another in moving closer to their shared purpose.

Soul groups are vibrationally attuned to awaken in unison, guided by the unique blueprint of their soul family. The specific soul family we are born into influences when we align with the one timeline.

The first soul groups to enter the one timeline are smaller and consist of those who begin to wake up earlier in the process. Larger groups follow later as the collective shift progresses. When all members of a soul group enter the one timeline, the entire group undergoes a significant vibrational upgrade, advancing together as a unified field. Throughout this process, we may encounter members of our soul group who show up in our lives, seemingly out of nowhere. These individuals may connect with us briefly to receive upgrades through our interactions or to provide us with necessary shifts. Interestingly, they may not seem to resonate with us at all, yet their presence serves a purpose before they move on. This intricate system facilitates growth and alignment within the group.

Some members of a soul group may already be in the one timeline, while others are not yet vibrationally ready. Until every member in the soul group has attained the one-timeline vibration, that soul group cannot fully embody the next vibrational shift. However, the universal mind orchestrates synchronicities that guide those who are not yet in the one timeline toward vibrational coherence. As more members of the group transition, the remaining members are naturally increasingly drawn in, ensuring the collective evolution of the soul group. Once all the members of that soul group have attained the one-timeline vibration the soul group can now fully embody a higher vibration that catapults the group into a highly advanced quantum Body. The soul group members can live geographically all over the planet and may never meet each other and we may be in contact with many of the soul members and even be partners with them. Consequently, we will see individuals completely unaware of any awakening, alongside those who possess a profound inner knowing beyond anything we have witnessed before.

For this reason, there are no "chosen ones."
We are all chosen, each playing an integral role in the
collective journey toward Unity and awakening. Anyone
proclaiming themselves as "being one of the chosen ones"
misunderstands this truth, as such declarations
often stem from ego rather than genuine alignment.
Trust instead in the wisdom that acknowledges
the shared and equal potential within all beings.

A paradigm shift of this magnitude cannot occur all at once. It
necessitates a balanced, incremental unfolding, allowing each
group to prepare the energetic foundation for those who
follow. Remarkably, the final groups to transition into the
one-timeline will do so with the least resistance, making their
shift smoother and more easeful. These individuals, often the
most oppressed and the least expected to embody Unity, will
reveal their light right when we need it most. These soul
groups will be massive in size, they will serve as powerful
catalysts, completing the collective shift and demonstrating
that no one is excluded from the journey into Unity!

The first soul group to enter the one-timeline will begin to
emerge as leaders and guides. Some will appear unexpectedly,
while others may have been in plain sight all along. The
collective influence of a soul group in raising the global
vibration cannot be overstated. Instead of a single enlightened
being, we will witness an entire wave of awakened individuals
rising together. That time is approaching, marking the point
where the separation paradigm will begin to rapidly implode.

As this unfolds, the next soul group will begin to coalesce,
continuing the wave of awakening within the one timeline.
Each soul group is larger than the last. This profound shift will
occur simultaneously across the planet, deeply altering the
collective vibration. Rather than inciting fear or panic, it will
bring an overwhelming sense of relief. The orchestration of

this awakening ensures that old patterns of divisions will resolve—whether religious, political, or societal- as all humanity rises together in Unity.

The realization that we are connected to a soul group strengthens our sense of community and eases feelings of isolation. Nature has orchestrated this transition in such a way that it cannot be extinguished. From this perspective, we can finally see that the paradigm shift is unstoppable. There is safety in numbers, and these awakened individuals will be present in all aspects of society—from those experiencing homelessness to those holding the highest positions in government.

Herbal Insights: Blue Lotus & Tulsi ☽

☽ **Blue Lotus** – The Celestial Unifier
Blue Lotus carries the essence of spiritual awakening, expanded consciousness, and deep inner harmony. Revered in ancient Egyptian and Vedic traditions, this sacred flower opens the third eye, enhances meditation, and invites divine connection. It is often associated with Unity consciousness, aligning personal energy with cosmic rhythms.
☽ ☽ Blue Lotus can be brewed into tea, smoked in ceremonial practice, or infused into oil for anointing before meditation or celestial alignments. Its presence bridges the seen and unseen, lifting awareness into higher vibrational states.

☽ **Tulsi** – The Heart's Sacred Guardian
Tulsi, or Holy Basil, is a sacred herb known for its ability to open the heart, clear emotional blockages, and deepen spiritual devotion. Cherished in Ayurveda as a plant of protection and purification, Tulsi harmonizes the body and mind, encouraging a state of loving presence.

☽ ☽ Enjoy Tulsi as a tea, in herbal baths, or as an anointing oil before heart-centered practices. Its gentle yet powerful essence restores balance, inviting warmth, clarity, and a deeper connection to self and spirit. ☽ ✦

CHAPTER NINETEEN

QUANTUM HUMAN

WE EXIST WITHIN THE REALM OF INFINITE POTENTIAL
&
INFINITE POTENTIAL EXISTS WITHIN US.

The one-timeline changes everything starting at the cellular level. Up until now, we have only been engaging with a very small percentage of the intelligence of the human body's guidance system. This is soon to change... The "now" is here! It is time we stop pretending that the paradigm shift isn't real or is beyond this lifetime in some far distant future. For many people, the shift is here—tangible right now. As we begin to experience these truths through our advanced inner knowing and immense life changes, the cast slowly unravels. We quench our thirst by drinking from the boundless well of Unity that lives within us. After the first sip—the taste of pure potential—we will feel an inner shift take root. Our wise body sends a message to remind us of our vast bio-communication system, poised and ready to come online.

In nature, we see evolution as a gradual process, a step by step unfolding over time. This understanding is deeply ingrained, which makes it difficult to fathom how humanity could transform in a few decades the equivalent of thousands of years of evolution.

The human body has been reimagined as a galactic hybrid, crafted to operate at a conscious, interdimensional level. Our transformation is not a distant event, but the unveiling of our quantum body—an unfolding driven by the Love and Divinity within. This process cannot be halted. In this metamorphosis, we transcend the sense of separation that has become embedded in our physical being. The healing of our collective and individual selves is nearing completion.

We have navigated the birth canal of transformation, faced the darkness of our shadow, and surrendered to the unknown. Through countless leaps of faith, we have arrived here. It is now time to pause, take a deep breath, and witness the Divine spark within.

We can rest at last—
Supported by the nourishing embrace of
the great Mother's Love.

As cellular regeneration unfolds, the rising vibrational energy supports a profound transformation at every level, allowing us to maintain emotional balance, heart-mind coherence, and a sense of inner harmony amidst the current planetary chaotic node. We find ourselves moving in and out of the neutrality of Love with greater ease. The lightness of this vibration is sweet, creative, playful, innately safe, and wildly abundant. Welcome home!

When we step out of autopilot,
we reconnect with our true nature—
one aligned with Unity & Divine purpose.

Now, we can embody the truth that we are indeed safe. The brain's neuroplasticity begins to increase exponentially at this juncture.This is the light at the end of the metaphysical tunnel. Everything improves more than we could have ever imagined... And when we believe in this possibility it happens even more so and with greater ease.

We begin to cultivate trust in ways we have never been able to in the past. From this place of enhanced inner knowing we take control of our healthcare. Our breath, voice, movement, sexuality, thought, and touch are truly holistic and biomechanical tools for maintaining health in the body. As we evolve, this truth becomes second nature. This is where we really begin to turn the corner and the separation paradigm begins to implode from within us. Body intelligence guides us to dissolve the origin seed of any dis-ease from inception and we actually listen and believe it and then we take action through physical form, our bodily mechanics.

As we cultivate a new somatic reality—one rooted in listening to the body—a new level of body awareness arises within our inner knowing in the form of conscious, intercellular communication. In turn, the reduced stress on the immune system strengthens it. Cuts and bones heal so quickly that most infections never even have the chance to manifest. We begin to have an abundance of energy! We realize we need less sleep and food to sustain our bodies than we previously thought. When our meals are nutrient dense we eat smaller quantities and require less energy to digest.

From the hot ashes of separation beliefs,
the Unity belief system rises & the fundamental belief
"I am safe" is solidified.

When we enter resonance with the one-timeline vibration, we experience an extraordinary level of vibrational protection—it's as though we become untouchable. At first, this may seem subtle, but over time awareness of this profound phenomena arises. This realization opens the door to cellular activation and the reawakening of morphogenetic codes that have long been dormant.

This is where the experience becomes exhilarating. As our cellular vibration rises, the body itself becomes a unified, coalesced system—a living quantum processor of Divine flow. This activation increases the flow of information and grants access to knowledge that feels both ancient and new.

With this newly freed energy, our cells' microtubules gain their full potential to process quantum information. Released from the limitations of time, these quantum structures can interpret the past, present, and future simultaneously—they are no longer dependent on linear organization.

An influx of interdimensional data reshapes the brain, expanding its neuroplasticity in ways that are nearly immeasurable. Trillions of new neural connections are formed as synapses strengthen and dendritic branches expand. The brain begins to process information directly from the Unified Field, bypassing traditional cognitive filters.

As the Feminine and Masculine energies unite harmoniously, we find ourselves in a grounded, peaceful state of heightened awareness. This super-conscious reality is focused on a grounded pragmatic purpose and a creative flow that consistently generates solutions for our lives that are in service to the whole. These changes will not happen all at once; however, we will likely notice a heightened sense of inner knowing beginning to emerge.

Let's be clear: We are not an AI system. We have human souls and hearts. We experience emotions and physical intimacy. We are a unique species and within us carry incredible capabilities. When we align with the Love vibration and with the Divine flow of nature, we begin to leap into a harmonious existence that is steeped in abundance.

That time is now!

In regard to the advanced Unity paradigm heart-mind coherence, the way we manifest drastically changes. How we love one another changes. The nature of every relationship is utterly altered. The decisions we make are no longer rooted in fear. Fear not! We have the knowledge of Divinity within us. From this knowing, we can perceive future timelines while making decisions. This does not imply we are not spontaneous or we do not make mistakes. It's just that we are now making decisions from a place of truth and in connection to all of nature and therefore are more likely to see the web of causality.

We are now able to access any pertinent information we may need for purpose at will. We will no longer be subject to external manipulation and we will solely embody beliefs that are built on the truth of our Divinity. We will live within embodied spiritual sovereignty. The need to defend our point of view diminishes as we understand that the ultimate Divine is sharing a piece of the puzzle through all of us—keys for each other's evolution and to encourage collective cooperation. The ego also shifts into a support mechanism to help foster a balanced, healthy self esteem.

This marks the moment when the boundary between humans and technology dissolves. With the body's bio-communication system fully activated, the need for devices like cell phones and laptops will diminish. Instead, we will communicate directly with other individual's biofields through the quantum mechanics of our physical and energetic beings.

This ability will extend beyond human interactions to include communication with animals, plants, and even interdimensional beings—if we choose to engage with them. This shift will not render verbal speech obsolete and in fact may evolve spoken language into something far more enriched—a nuanced and sophisticated form of communication capable of conveying more complex layers of meaning, emotions, and multidimensional experiences that our language has previously fallen short to express.

We will develop the ability to share images and ideas directly—showing others vivid scenes, thoughts, and locations in ways that far surpass the current limitations of our devices. This new form of communication will be effortless, instantaneous, and more immersive than anything we have known before.

As this happens, humans will begin to step into their quantum potential. Alongside this growth, biological quantum computers will emerge. These systems will not require invasive implants or neural chips; instead, they will merge with us as natural extensions of our biofields. Their primary purpose will be to handle routine and menial tasks, creating seamless a dynamic between human and technology.

These "next-generation computers" will be forms of natural technology fully connected to the Unified Field, just as we are. This intrinsic connection will make them immune to corruption and capable of evolving alongside humanity. We will be able to communicate with them intuitively, directing their functions with ease as they carry out tasks without requiring our direct involvement.

This transformation will inevitably lead to the replacement of many current jobs, yet it will also redefine our entire concept of work. Roles that once shaped the modern world will become obsolete, creating space for new avenues of purpose, creativity, and exploration.

This is a shift we will need to face collectively. By this stage, the fear of survival—the primary force that has driven many of our systems—will be nearly eradicated. Many of the jobs that humans have taken part in for decades are actually better suited for AI. We are not machines—we are designed to create, connect, and thrive.

Industries such as government, policing, military, healthcare, education, construction, wall street, energy, and manufacturing systems will all undergo radical change. The traditional five-day workweek will no longer be relevant as humanity steps into a new rhythm of purpose driven action and rest.

Give yourself some time to process all of this as these notions may first come as a surprise, feel unsettling, or on the contrary feel wildly invigorating and exciting. As with everything, gleen what resonates and leave the rest.

It may feel challenging or foreign to imagine what we would do with our time without the constraints of our current jobs. This is an understandable inquiry since many of us have never even tasted a different reality or rhythm of life. We will not be aimlessly laying around. We will have Divine purpose and accordingly aligned tasks to accomplish.

As we raise the body's vibration we will no longer want to work jobs that lack purpose or contribute to the destruction of our previous ecosystem. Trust that as all of this unfolds it will make more sense. There is a plan.

As we awaken to the potential of the quantum body, a vast realm of untapped possibilities open up. We gain access to the creation of natural technologies that only manifest at higher frequencies of consciousness. Such innovations require Unity and trust. And without such qualities, said advancements could be misused by lower level energies (i.e., the separation paradigm).

Through trusting in ourselves and honoring the Divinity within, we open the door to boundless and free energy, advanced healthcare systems based on vibrational medicine, and natural technologies capable of transforming our cities into thriving ecosystems of harmony and innovation.

We have shifted away from scarcity based mindsets—beliefs that resources are limited and that life is a competition—and embraced a consciousness of benevolent abundance that prioritizes collective well-being and creativity.

This heightened awareness reveals how intricately woven we are into the fabric of nature and with one another, as though understanding and connection occur through a process similar to osmosis. We no longer see ourselves as separate from the natural world, but as equal participants in a shared web of life.

This recognition of equality begins to radically shift the way we interact with the world. As we come to see the sacredness in everything, that reverence becomes reflected in our external reality. We crave deep, meaningful relationships, placing connection and community at the heart of our lives. In this flow state, the notion of outsourcing our roles—such as letting others raise our children—feels increasingly out of harmony with our values. Instead, we embrace the interconnectedness of life and the importance of shared stewardship for the generations to come.

As we align more closely with this pure, natural rhythm, our use of energy becomes intentional and mindful. We are no longer driven by urgency or constant productivity. Rather, we are guided by a slower, more harmonious pace that honors the present moment. Life becomes an unfolding—a sacred experience where each simple moment carries profound meaning. We see the mundane as sacred. In this state of being, we remember that everything and everyone is and has always been sacred. It is only now, in this new paradigm, that we are fully able to live in accordance with this truth. This shift allows us to cultivate a world where connection, care, and reverence are central to how we live, create, and grow together.

Herbal Insights: Rhodiola ☽

☽ **Best Ways to Use:** Tincture, capsule, tea infusion, or
meditation support.

🌿 **Rhodiola (Rhodiola rosea) – The Adaptogenic Key
for Cellular Transition & Telepathic Activation**
Rhodiola is a potent adaptogen known for strengthening the
nervous system,

☽ **Key Benefits:**

Supports Cellular Adaptation – Helps the body integrate
energetic shifts smoothly.Enhances Brainwave Coherence –
Increases alpha and gamma wave activity, essential for
telepathic receptivity. Boosts Mitochondrial Function –
Provides sustained cellular energy for higher vibrational
states. Stabilizes the Nervous System – Prevents burnout
while expanding perception.

☽ **Ways to Connect:**

Tincture or Capsule – Take in the morning for sustained
energy and adaptability. Tea Infusion – Brew Rhodiola root
with honey for grounding and expansion. Meditation Support
– Pair with breathwork or heart coherence practices for
deeper energetic alignment.

CHAPTER TWENTY

THE GOLDEN TIMELINE

PURE GOLDEN LIGHT OF AWAKENING.

The Golden Timeline, much like the one-timeline, serves as the final bridge to the Unity paradigm. However, unlike the one-timeline, which reflects an individual's inner harmonic convergence, the Golden Timeline signals a shared moment of collective awakening. Obviously this collective shift is yet to take place. To be clear, this is not a miraculous moment where a magical wand instantly heals our ecosystem or purifies Earth of all toxins. We cannot simply step into a parallel universe to escape the consequences of what we, as a collective, have contributed to over time. Nevertheless, the Golden Timeline creates a massive spark when we shift into its golden light.

This massive human leap into the unknown will occur once all humans have entered into the one-timeline vibration. By then, all soul groups will have fully entered and we, as a species, will be prepared to embody the Golden Timeline vibration with ease. Our collective and individual belief structures will have shifted, since we will have already integrated much of the Unity vibration. The external systems we once naïvely depended on, will have begun to implode. Millions upon millions of humans will have already embodied an elevated vibration that exponentially raises the frequency of the collective. Individuals will have navigated the chaotic nodes that led them to advanced biological upgrades—deepening their understanding of both the collective human purpose and their unique individual purpose.

This mass shift will Yes, it will happen all at once. In a single, transformative moment—a giant spark of divine awakening—we will collectively enter the Golden Timeline. From that moment forward, nothing will ever be the same. We will awaken to our shared purpose: to merge with nature in a mass remembrance, with each other, and with the universal flow of life. Together, we will dismantle outdated systems that no longer serve us and reconstruct a new world inspired by the wisdom of nature and the principles of biomimicry.

268

Biomimicry teaches us to look to nature, which has spent billions of years honing the art of balance, harmony, and resiliency. By emulating these natural structures, we can design systems, technologies, and ways of living that are not only sustainable but highly regenerative. In the Golden Timeline, every aspect of human life will be realigned with the rhythms of the Earth, ensuring that we thrive in Unity with our planet.

Like the wisdom of nature, these advanced systems would seamlessly adapt to their environments, offering clean and abundant power while preserving Earth's delicate balance. Imagine free energy technologies inspired by innate toroidal fields, replicating the self-sustaining energy flows found in living cells and the magnetic fields that surround and sustain all life. These universal energy systems hold the potential to transform how we power our world, creating solutions that are not only efficient but also align with the natural rhythms of existence.

Harnessing these systems requires integrating biotechnology with the foundational principles of toroidal fields. In doing so, we will unlock groundbreaking possibilities for sustainable energy. Such innovation calls for interdisciplinary and non-competitive collaboration—cross pollination—between physics, biology, and engineering to bring these concepts to life—for these flowers to bloom. These technologies will emerge effortlessly, in alignment with the quantum Universal mind, operating on vibrational principles that resonate with the interwoven fabric of reality itself.

This type of self-sustaining energy will fulfill all of our energy needs without reliance on wires, cell towers, or other disruptive infrastructure. It offers a vision of a world where energy flows freely and harmoniously, mirroring the regenerative processes of nature, and empowers humanity to coexist in balance—in Unity—with the Earth.

Within the Golden Timeline, our built environments will also transform. Picture alive, breathing buildings that are designed with the principles of sacred geometry. They will appear luminescent and the interiors will be just as beautiful as any modern home. They will be connected to the Earth in ways that foster optimal health for the inhabitants. The flow of energy within these structures will provide clear communication to our inner knowing as there will be no electrical lines or artificial electromagnetic waves in the environment that could interfere.

These structures will be constructed from biodegradable, non-toxic materials like algae, fungi, or hemp and thus will support their surroundings by purifying the air, recycling water, and being a habitat for plants. These living buildings will connect human spaces to the Earth's energetic grid—creating harmony between our built environment and the natural world.

As cities are dismantled, they will simultaneously be rebuilt to flow harmoniously with nature. Waterways, animal corridors, and regenerative ecosystems will become integral parts of urban design. We will no longer need to "escape" into nature because we will always be living in connection with it, surrounded by its rhythms and vitality. These new cities will honor the sacred balance of life, allowing humanity to thrive as an integrated part of the natural world.

This is a balanced feminine & masculine scientific world— the ultimate Unity reality.

On an even greater scale, the soil itself will be healed. By studying the way plants, fungi, and microbes work together, we can implement permanent solutions to combat desertification. For example, planting drought-resistant native
270

trees and vegetation stabilizes soil and increases water retention. Water-harvesting innovations inspired by desert organisms as well as soil-enrichment approaches such as biochar and introducing mycelium, will aid Earth's regeneration. This is learning from and applying the wisdom of nature! These efforts will not only restore biodiversity, but will also absorb carbon dioxide, cool the climate, and increase habitats for generations to come.

From this point forth, we will support the regeneration of Earth's foundation beneath the soil instead of challenging its survival as we have in the separation paradigm. Mycelium networks possess remarkable communication pathways as well as break down organic matter and distribute nutrients to plants. They offer a clear blueprint for soil restoration. By integrating the old, wise practices of no-till farming, composting, and biochar into our agricultural techniques we will create rich soils that sequester carbon and ensure food security for all. Cultivating the land and growing food creates the ultimate connection and Unity with life. The days of corporate farming will be over!

Each transformation of the Golden Timeline is woven together by the collective need to reconnect to the plant "kindom." Nature has always shown us the way forward and yet under recent illusions we lost this connection. The natural world thrives because it operates in cycles—regenerative, balanced, and deeply cooperative. In the Golden Timeline, we will embrace the feminine wisdom and flow along with the strength and structure brought forth by the masculine. From this balanced state we will humbly create systems that mirror these natural principles in every facet of life.

The Golden Timeline is not an implausible dream—it is our rapidly approaching reality! It marks the awakening of humanity to our Divine potential and collective purpose. It is the moment of remembering—on a cellular level—that we are the stewards of this Earth. That we are the co-creators of the future—where everything we build, grow, and do is a reflection of the harmony innate to nature.

If it has not yet been clearly stated, let us emphasize that we are NOT going back to what we used to believe and how we used to function. While the wisdom of the ancients will be forever within us, we are moving into a natural, technological era of highly advanced evolutionary times. It may be tempting to think that returning to a simpler way of life—living off the land as indigenous peoples once did—is the answer... But this is not where we are headed.

This new era is not about reverting to old ways, but about evolving into a state of balance where technology, nature, and humanity are interconnected in Unity. We are entering a new paradigm where we honor the lessons of the past, while simultaneously embracing a future where advanced technology seamlessly coexists with nature. Moreover, we ourselves are the advanced technology—deeply resonant with the solutions continuously emerging from the universal mind. It cannot be overstated how effortlessly change can occur when we exist in a state of unity vibration. Without fear or scarcity blocking the flow of innovation, new ideas and creations come through us with ease. In this state, we become the communication systems that were once external, embodying the connectivity and intelligence that mirrors the natural world.

Upon reading this passage, what is the dominant thought and felt sense in the body?

Is there a secondary thought or feeling?

Sit with this for a few minutes. Allow all the reasons that this seems impossible to flood your system.

272

Once again, this shift will happen all at once. We will collectively enter the Golden Timeline in a single, transformative moment—a giant spark of Divine awakening. And from that moment forward, nothing will ever be the same.

Imagine a world without war. A world where resources are not wasted on the destruction of life. Without wars, there would be significantly less lingering trauma, no ripple effects of violence causing dis-ease in mind, body, or spirit. Imagine a world where sexual violence no longer existed. A world where healing is the natural state, not a costly, exclusive privilege.

Now, consider what would happen if the food we ate nourished us completely—if every bite came from nutrient-dense, organically grown plants and animals raised in Unity with the Earth. If the water we drank was pure, free of toxins, and as clean as the springs that flow through the wilderness. Without the burden of chronic illness caused by poor diets and environmental toxins, our bodies will thrive and our spirits will soar.

What if we no longer had to pay utility bills, phone bills, or other artificially imposed necessities? Imagine a world where free, renewable energy powers our homes, and we ourselves become the communication systems. In the quantum reality of the Golden Timeline, external quantum computers are seamlessly connected within us. With our fully functioning quantum brain, we can interact with these systems effortlessly, guiding and requesting their service. What if this interconnected technology was as accessible and natural as breathing, harmonizing with our lives in profound and transformative ways? What if the magnitude of governments shrank to a trace of what it is today? Imagine governments no longer being intrusive and overbearing systems of control, but organizations that truly support and nourish communities?

Without the need for invasive policies, fear-driven laws, or an ever-growing bureaucracy, people could live freely, guided by mutual respect and an innate sense of personal responsibility.

Imagine a world without the need for police, because our communities were safe by design and people's innate and soul needs were met, so the trigger for violence dissolved. A world where people lived in Unity with one another, free of fear, free of crime—a world where the systems that create desperation, inequality, and violence simply ceased to exist. In such a world, we would no longer feel unsafe because safety would be an inherent part of our shared reality.

What if the healthcare system were no longer a profit-driven menace? In a world of clean food, pure water, and a harmonious, reciprocal connection with nature, we would be empowered to heal ourselves. Ancient healthcare techniques, combined with this balance, could render chronic diseases obsolete. However, trauma care, broken bones, and emergencies would still require specialized attention. Imagine health centers evolving into smaller, integrated facilities, merging advanced technologies with natural, holistic care to provide a more balanced, compassionate approach to healing.

So, if all of these things were to be true, would we even need money? Think about it, money today exists largely to manage scarcity—scarcity of resources, scarcity of time, scarcity of opportunity. But in a world without war, without artificial scarcity, and without exploitative systems, the need for money would diminish... if not disappear entirely. People would no longer work for survival; they would work for passion, purpose, and the joy of creation. Instead of chasing wealth, we embody abundance and innately with enthusiasm follow fulfillment, collaboration, and connection.

Such a world would function through abundance. With nature as our guide, resources would flow freely, be shared, and be replenished in ways that mirror the regenerative cycles of the Earth. Communities would be built on cooperation and mutual support, rather than competition and profit. Every person would contribute their unique gifts not because they "have to," but because they want to. And in giving, they would receive tenfold—just as in nature.

This vision is not an impossible dream. It is the much needed return to the natural order of life. A world free from war, disease, and exploitation is not a utopia—it's what happens when humanity aligns itself with the flow of life. This is what happens when we let go of fear, scarcity, and control, and instead choose to embrace trust, abundance, and love.

None of this suggests that challenges will disappear. We will still live human lives, and relationship issues will arise. Failures and setbacks will remain part of our journey. Natural events, like floods and earthquakes, will still occur, and yes, we will still stub our toes from time to time. However, the overall energy will shift toward a positive, solution-based reality.

While we may occasionally find ourselves reminiscing about the days of living paycheck to paycheck, dealing with depression, and working through the weight of past traumas, those moments of nostalgia will be fleeting—lasting only a few minutes before we return to the brighter, more harmonious reality we've co-created.

As we awaken to the potential of the quantum body, a vast realm of new possibilities emerge. Here we gain access to the creation of natural technologies that can only manifest at higher frequencies of consciousness. These technologies require the feminine and masculine energy to be balanced for this highly elevated information to be revealed. These technologies are the extension of an evolved natural continuum that nourishes the ecosystem, never harming nature.

The technologies to arise within the Golden Timeline are a gift from the Divine, bestowed upon humanity to assist us in aligning with nature and the universal flow of life. In many ways, these technologies are already emerging. Many however, remain dormant due to the constraints of the separation paradigm—a paradigm that tightly controls external systems, suppresses innovation, and restricts potential.

The origin seeds of Divine technologies are waiting patiently for the shift, ready to sprout as humanity collectively awakens. While some of these seeds have already begun to germinate—new life emerging from the cracks of old systems—the revolutionary advancements we have witnessed thus far are merely the tip of the iceberg. The Golden Timeline will initiate an unstoppable flood of breakthroughs—an explosion of innovations—that harmonize humanity with the Earth and the cosmos.

Awakened beings will not seek to exploit these emergent, natural super powerful technologies for personal or material gain. Unlike the old paradigm—which commodified and weaponized innovation—those living in the Golden Timeline will understand the sacred nature of these gifts. They will honor their Divine origins, using them to serve the greater good, uplift humanity, and heal our connection to nature and all of life.

These technologies will neither dominate, nor control. Rather, they will integrate seamlessly into the natural order, working in harmony with the cycles and the elements. Innovations born within the Golden Timeline will arise from love, Unity, and a profound sense of stewardship, not from illusion, ego, or greed. As tools of liberation—not domination—these free energy systems are inspired by nature's flow and thus regenerate and heal the body from the cellular level.

276

As the separation paradigm crumbles and the Golden Timeline takes root, we can rest assured that the seeds of innovation will flourish—breaking free of the constraints that have long kept them dominant. Next, comes a miraculous and revolutionary wave of technologies that are equally sacred as they are transformative. Awakening us to new possibilities, they will utterly dismantle the current infrastructures and pave the way for our new reality to establish.

Of course there will be work to do. As we deconstruct the infrastructure of the separation paradigm, we will replace it with new cities and communities that align with the Unity Paradigm. Just as we have deconstructed our limiting belief systems and detoxified our bodies, creating space for Unity to rise within us, the same process of regeneration and rebuilding will occur in our external systems. The inner and outer transformations are deeply interconnected, each reflecting and reinforcing the other. Nature will guide us—offering solutions to compost nuclear waste, neutralize chemical compounds like plastics in the ocean, and clear pharmaceuticals from our drinking water. With our expanded awareness of the Unity Paradigm, we will understand that all substances are vibrational in nature. So, for every problem, there is a vibrational counterpart capable of transforming even the most toxic materials into a harmless or even beneficial form. This new orientation to following nature, versus imposing our ideas, allows us to create from nature's intelligence and thus heal the planet in profound ways.

The rebuilding of the external world is one of the primary purposes of the Golden Timeline. Before we can fully live within the Unity Paradigm, our external structures must mirror the internal awakening that is taking place within us. Together, we will create a reality where every system—whether technological, social, or ecological—reflects the harmony, vibrancy, and interconnectedness of life itself.

The one-timeline will bring every human being into a state of harmonic convergence, uniting all of humanity in a shared purpose for this great reconstruction—this return to Divine truth. In this new reality, the energy from all humans will flow in coherence. As we each fulfill our unique role in the regeneration of our world's infrastructure, scarcity will diminish and we will all have more than enough. There will not be an oppressive government commanding our involvement in the regeneration. Instead, we will rebuild through Unity, trust, and our innate co-creative energy.

It may feel challenging to imagine how any of this will even be possible while living in the current climate of greed, competition, and scarcity. For this reason, we simply invite you to pause and imagine—even for a moment—what role you might play in this new timeline. If that feels too far fetched or unattainable, see if you can simply explore the origin seed within you—the seed tucked just below the surface in your soil-soul waiting to emerge. Whether you believe it or not, your seed is an integral part of this new reality coming into existence. When it is nurtured, it will grow into your unique—and necessary—contribution to the harmony, abundance, and regeneration of life on Earth.

The human race was designed to enter this new era together. It is not by accident that we are living at this pivotal juncture—it is our Divine purpose to aid our collective evolution. We were not placed here as a destructive force, but rather as stewards of the planet able to rapidly evolve when the time is right. And this moment is nearing!

Our collective purpose is clear

Awaken in unison and align with the natural world to protect and restore the delicate balance of the ecosystem.

In this shared awakening, billions of us will merge into a unified consciousness, thereby diminishing the chaos of entropy and strengthening coherence across the collective field.

This reset sends ripples through the elemental patterns of existence. Water—the primal carrier of life and memory—reflects this instant shift, amplifying the harmonious resonance throughout the entire planet. As Water resets, it acts as a conductor of the new vibration, facilitating the symbiosis between humanity and the natural world. In this unified state, all of nature mirrors this transformation—trees sway with new vitality, animals instinctively respond to the harmonious rhythm, and the air itself hums with balance.

The simultaneous awakening of billions of humans experiencing their true nature and activating their quantum body will inevitably send a surge of energy into the Earth's toroidal field. Since we are part of and one with this field, this radical shift will disrupt the previous leakage of energy. The energy that previously was being siphoned off into external systems will no longer be a concern. All toroidal fields of the Earth and of individuals will be contained, no longer experiencing the loss of vital source energy. The immense power from billions of awakened humans will surge through all elements of Earth, activating and clearing all planetary gateways. In this state of coherence, the heart of the planet mirrors the high vibrational frequency of awakened beings, thereby creating a feedback loop that strengthens the bond between humanity and nature. This is not a forced shift, but an organic unfolding—a sacred restoration of balance and connection.

The timing of this event will likely correlate with the weakening of Earth's magnetic field and an even greater galactic event. As Earth's toroidal field is strengthened, the mass extinction timeline will be resolved as a new elemental pattern is created and the Unity timeline is solidified.

This is the paradigm shift.

It has always been the collective purpose of the human species to be a catalyst for change on the galactic level. Through awakened body's and the clearing of the gateways, we collectively ignite the spark. By waking up simultaneously, we will create a spark large enough to alter the course of the current mass extinction elemental pattern. To inhibit the healing of that timeline, the evolutionary flow was slowed. However, since the origin seed of Unity was embedded within our DNA thousands of years ago we embody the potential for great change. To embody this truth all we need to do is to explore how we ourselves are moving through this process on the micro personal level it is the same on the planetary and galactic level it is the same awakening and evolutionary resolution. The immense collective chaotic node we have been experiencing since the inception of the Unity paradigm is finally concluding. We are waking up—soon the storm of evolution will settle.

Take pause. Give yourself time to reflect on the significance and immense complexity of this radical return to a more *true* state of being.

Once in the Golden Timeline

After experiencing the massive collective spark that resolved the mass extinction and created the golden Timeline, many of us will go through a period of integration. During this phase, it is important to understand that while our physical surroundings may initially appear unchanged, the true transformation happens within us. Our relationship with collective energies begins to shift rapidly, sparking an exponential moment of accelerated vibrational frequency. This heightened state accelerates our evolutionary growth and reshapes our perception of reality as well as the dynamic flow of time.

In this vibration, humanity moves steadily toward the full realization and embodiment of the Unity paradigm. Here, our actions, thoughts, and intentions no longer stem from a need to heal or correct perceived imbalance. Instead, they flow effortlessly in harmony with the whole. The struggle for connection and the urge to repair give way to a new state of being in the moment—a complete trust that dissolves doubt. In this state, we no longer seek constant validation or empirical evidence; we simply know when the information we receive is authentic and real.

Our sense of time changes—our bodies live longer and the cellular structure cycle elongates. We are living in a newly formed and stable mathematical equation. This new state stabilizes the chaotic node we have been living in and prepares us for the ultimate Unity paradigm shift

While it may feel nearly impossible to envision such a reality in the midst of current chaos, the possibility exists. By slightly cracking the door, we allow light to pour in and thus begin to experience this new mode of being. Any lingering beliefs rooted in separation—whether from past lives, soul imprints, family dynamics, individual traumatic patterns, or collective separation patterns—will be instantly resolved as we enter the Golden Timeline, for such attachments cannot be sustained within this higher vibrational state. Karmic codes will be reset instantaneously. All elemental patterns left unresolved will be instantly resolved; we will not carry forth dis-ease on any level. New elemental patterns in Unity are born!

In this moment all water on Earth will embody a fifth-dimensional crystalline structure acting as a conduit for Unity and ultimate coherence. This profound reset allows us to collectively exhale—releasing the burdens of fragmentation—and entering a state of sheer peace and clarity.

Key Terms & Concepts

Resonant Frequency - refers to the natural frequency at which a system, object, or being vibrates most efficiently. When exposed to an external frequency that matches its own, the system absorbs energy more effectively, leading to amplified vibrations. This concept applies to physics, biology, and consciousness, influencing how energy flows through structures, from atoms and cells to sound waves and electromagnetic fields.

In human experience, resonant frequency can describe the alignment between our personal energy and external influences, such as emotions, thoughts, beliefs, elemental patterns, or environmental vibrations, affecting our well-being and perception of reality.

Resonance – The natural frequency at which energy or vibrations synchronize, creating harmony.

Sympathetic Resonance – When one vibrating system influences another to vibrate at the same frequency, reinforcing connection and alignment.

Entrainment – The synchronization of two energy systems, often seen in heart rates, brainwaves, and planetary rhythms.

Quantum Field – The infinite, interconnected energy field from which all matter, consciousness, and potential emerge.

Quantum Field Theory-A way of understanding the universe that treats all particles as ripples or excitations in underlying energy fields. Each type of particle is a different ripple in its own field—like light coming from the electromagnetic field. This theory is the backbone of modern physics and points to a reality where everything is energy in motion.

String Theory-A theoretical framework suggesting that the tiniest building blocks of the universe are not particles, but tiny vibrating strings of energy. These vibrations give rise to the different forms of matter and forces, like musical notes played on a single instrument. It attempts to unite gravity with quantum mechanics into one deeper theory of everything.

Unified Field-The invisible web of connection that unites all matter, energy, and consciousness into one living presence. It is the space where everything is part of everything else, beyond the illusion of separation. Often described as the source field, it carries the frequency of love and awareness and can be felt when we are deeply connected to ourselves, nature, and each other.

Ascension – A vibrational shift toward higher awareness, expanded consciousness, and the embodiment of Unity.

Coherence – The alignment of energy, emotions, and thought patterns into a state of balance and clarity.

Heart Coherence – A physiological and energetic state where the heart's electromagnetic field aligns with emotions, thoughts, and the nervous system, creating balance, resilience, and expanded consciousness.

Cymatics - Cymatics is the study of visible sound and vibration, typically observed through patterns formed in a medium such as water, sand, or other substances when exposed to specific frequencies. The term comes from the Greek word *kyma*, meaning "wave." Cymatics demonstrates how sound can organize matter into intricate geometric shapes, revealing the hidden structure of vibration in the physical world.

Toroidal Field – A self-sustaining, donut-shaped energy field that cycles energy continuously, seen in the body, Earth, and universe.

Gateways – Energy portals or transition points that facilitate shifts in consciousness, dimensional access, or energetic evolution.

Harmonic Convergence – A global energetic shift that occurs when celestial alignments or human collective consciousness create a moment of amplified resonance, allowing for planetary transformation and acceleration of spiritual awakening.

Unity – The awareness that all life is interconnected as part of a singular, harmonious whole.

Divine Union – The merging of masculine and feminine energies within the neutrality of love, sparking creation and transformation.

Paradigm – A framework of beliefs, assumptions, and perspectives that shape how reality is perceived.

Paradigm Shift – A fundamental transformation in awareness that alters perception and understanding and changes the vibration in the collective,

Inner Knowing is the direct connection to the Universal Mind, a constant exchange of divine intelligence where synchronicities align and timelines unfold effortlessly. It is the voice that speaks without words, a deep resonance with truth beyond logic—guidance that simply is.

Intuition is the body's way of listening, an energetic dialogue through the heart, gut, and nervous system. It's the pull, the pause, the sensation that guides in real-time, responding to subtle shifts in the unseen.

Shadow Self – The unconscious or repressed aspects of oneself that are often shaped by fear, trauma, or societal conditioning. Integrating the shadow self leads to greater wholeness and self-awareness.

Universal Mind – The infinite intelligence that connects and permeates all of existence, acting as the source of consciousness, wisdom, and creativity across all dimensions.

The Unknown – The vast, uncharted space beyond what is familiar, offering both uncertainty and limitless potential. Embracing the unknown allows for transformation, trust, and expansion into new possibilities.

Sacred Geometry – The universal patterns and mathematical structures that form the foundation of all life, reflected in nature, art, and spiritual systems.

Natural Algorithms – The self-organizing codes and sequences that govern life's patterns, seen in ecosystems, weather, and biological rhythms.

Embodiment – The practice of fully integrating higher consciousness into physical existence and daily actions.

Abundance – A state of infinite possibility and sufficiency, recognizing the universe as inherently generous.

Taking the Leap – The act of stepping into the unknown with trust, courage, and faith in the unfolding path. This leap often marks the beginning of a transformative journey and the expansion into new levels of consciousness.

Cellular Structure – The foundational organization of living beings at a microscopic level, influenced by frequency, intention, and consciousness.

Biomimicry – The practice of learning from and applying nature's designs and processes to create sustainable, life-enhancing systems.

Microtubules – Microscopic, cylindrical structures within cells, believed to play a role in consciousness by transmitting quantum information.

Divine – The sacred, infinite intelligence present in all existence.

Divinity – The inherent sacred essence within all beings and creation.

Our True Nature – The unconditioned essence of being, rooted in love, unity, and infinite expansion.

Free Will – The inherent ability to make conscious choices independent of external forces, shaping one's reality through intention, belief, and action. True free will flourishes when aligned with Unity and the flow of Divine Love.

Metamorphosis – The profound transformation of an individual or collective, shifting from one state of being to another, often through a deep process of surrender and emergence into a new form.

Quantum Field – The infinite, interconnected energy field from which all matter, consciousness, and potential emerge.

Quantum Field Theory-A way of understanding the universe that treats all particles as ripples or excitations in underlying energy fields. Each type of particle is a different ripple in its own field—like light coming from the electromagnetic field. This theory is the backbone of modern physics and points to a reality where everything is energy in motion.

String Theory-A theoretical framework suggesting that the tiniest building blocks of the universe are not particles, but tiny vibrating strings of energy. These vibrations give rise to the different forms of matter and forces, like musical notes played on a single instrument. It attempts to unite gravity with quantum mechanics into one deeper theory of everything.

Unified Field-The invisible web of connection that unites all matter, energy, and consciousness into one living presence. It is the space where everything is part of everything else, beyond the illusion of separation. Often described as the source field, it carries the frequency of love and awareness and can be felt when we are deeply connected to ourselves, nature, and each other.

Cymatics - Cymatics is the study of visible sound and vibration, typically observed through patterns formed in a medium such as water, sand, or other substances when exposed to specific frequencies. The term comes from the Greek word *kyma*, meaning "wave." Cymatics demonstrates how sound can organize matter into intricate geometric shapes, revealing the hidden structure of vibration in the physical world.

The Neutrality of Love – The purest state of love, existing beyond polarity, judgment, or attachment. It is the all-encompassing presence that fuels creation, sustains life, and allows for divine transformation.

Zero Point – The state of absolute balance and potential, often described as the stillness between forces. In quantum physics, it refers to the lowest energy state of a system, where fluctuations still occur despite the absence of external energy. In metaphysical thought, it represents a space of pure neutrality, where transformation and infinite possibility emerge.

Non-Locality – The principle that objects or events can be connected regardless of distance, transcending traditional notions of space and time. In quantum physics, non-locality refers to the phenomenon where particles can instantaneously influence each other, no matter how far apart they are, as demonstrated in quantum entanglement. In metaphysical perspectives, it suggests that consciousness and energy are interconnected beyond physical limitations.

Reading list

The Quantum Brain – Jeffrey Satinover (2001) Explores the intersection of quantum mechanics and neuroscience, discussing how quantum theory may influence our understanding of consciousness and brain function.

The HeartMath Solution – Doc Childre and Howard Martin (1999) Introduces the HeartMath system, emphasizing the heart's role in emotional well-being and offering techniques to harness heart intelligence for improved health and stress management.

The Magdalene Manuscript – Tom Kenyon and Judi Sion (2002) A channeled text offering insights into the life of Mary Magdalene, her relationship with Jesus, and ancient Egyptian alchemy practices for spiritual transformation.

The Field – Lynne McTaggart (2001) Investigates the concept of the Zero Point Field, suggesting that a vast energy field connects all living things and influences consciousness and reality.

The Biology of Belief – Bruce H. Lipton (2005) Explores how beliefs and perceptions impact cellular function, proposing that thoughts and emotions can influence genetic expression and overall health.

Quantum Enigma – Bruce Rosenblum and Fred Kuttner (2006) Examines the paradoxes of quantum mechanics, particularly how observation appears to affect physical reality, with implications for consciousness and free will.

Biomimicry: Innovation Inspired by Nature – Janine M. Benyus (1997) Explores how nature's designs and processes inspire sustainable innovations in technology, architecture, and medicine.

The Holographic Universe – Michael Talbot (1991) Proposes that the universe functions as a hologram, where each part contains the whole, offering explanations for paranormal phenomena and consciousness.

The Structure of Scientific Revolutions – Thomas S. Kuhn (1962)

Introduces the concept of paradigm shifts, describing how scientific progress occurs through revolutionary changes in fundamental frameworks of thought.

Shadows of the Mind: A Search for the Missing Science of Consciousness – Roger Penrose (1994)

Argues that current science cannot fully explain consciousness and suggests quantum processes within the brain may play a fundamental role.

Consciousness and the Universe: Quantum Physics, Evolution, Brain & Mind – Stuart Hameroff, Roger Penrose, and Henry P. Stapp (2011)

A collection of essays exploring the relationship between quantum physics and consciousness, discussing how quantum processes may underlie cognition and awareness.

Taking the Leap: Freeing Ourselves from Old Habits and Fears – Pema Chödrön (2009)

Offers guidance on breaking free from negative habits and fears, encouraging mindfulness and compassion as tools for transformation.

Secrets of the Talking Jaguar: A Mayan Shaman's Journey to the Heart of the Indigenous Soul – Martín Prechtel (1998)

A memoir of the author's experiences living among the Tzutujil Maya people in Guatemala, sharing insights into their spiritual traditions and shamanic teachings.

"The Epigenetics Revolution" – Nessa Carey (2012) A great introduction to how genes can be influenced by external factors like stress, diet, and environment.

"Epigenetics" – C. David Allis, Thomas Jenuwein, Danny Reinberg, & Marie-Laure Caparros (2007) A foundational book on the science of epigenetics, co-authored by leading researchers in the field.

"The Source Field Investigations" – David Wilcock (2011) Explores the Zero Point Field in relation to consciousness, energy, and ancient knowledge.

"Zero Point Energy: The Fuel of the Future" – Thomas Valone (2007, updated edition) Examines scientific and technological theories related to harnessing zero-point energy.

"Mary Magdalene Revealed" – Meggan Watterson (2019) Explores the hidden wisdom of Mary Magdalene, offering insights into sacred love, divine union, and the balance of masculine and feminine energies.

.

www.ingramcontent.com/pod-product-compliance
Lightning Source LLC
Chambersburg PA
CBHW031944080426
42735CB00007B/251